Preface

"In this world, nothing can be said to be certain, except death and taxes." - Benjamin Franklin

In the tangled web of modern finance, where every decision seems both paramount and mystifying, it's tempting to retreat to the sidelines. Yet, Franklin's words remind us of the inexorable forces at play—taxes among them—and the undeniable necessity of navigating these waters with both wisdom and audacity. This book is your compass.

At its core, this guide is a voyage into the less charted territories of finance and wealth-building. It's crafted with the understanding that the journey to financial freedom is not merely about saving—it's about strategically amplifying your assets. Our expedition will traverse through the intricate landscapes of savvy investing and tactical tax planning. We'll delve deep into the realms of option securities, convertible debentures, and untapped real estate strategies, all while equipping you with the advanced tax techniques needed to shield your prospering wealth.

The impetus behind penning this guide was not merely to add to the cacophony of financial advice that fills our digital shelves. I was moved by stories of individuals just like you—ambitious, astute, yet tethered by the complexity of modern markets. Picture Sarah, a mid-level professional who, despite her proficiency in basic investments, felt paralyzed by the opaque nature of advanced financial instruments. Or, consider Michael, an entrepreneur whose dreams of a diversified portfolio were often dissipated by the daunting tax implications. Their stories resonated deeply, not just as missed opportunities, but as a clarion call for a navigational beacon in the financial labyrinth.

In charting this course, I was fortunate to be guided by the brilliant minds of fellow financial experts, alongside the sage advice of seasoned investors. Their collective wisdom, sharpened by the forge of experience, forms the backbone of this guide.

As you turn these pages, my hope is that you'll find more than just financial strategies. My aspiration is for you to discover a pathway to freedom—freedom from uncertainty, freedom to dream audaciously, and the freedom to achieve those dreams. I'm grateful for the slice of your life you're investing in my work, and I don't take that lightly.

This book is for you if you're ready to elevate your understanding of financial investments beyond the entry-level, if you seek not just to navigate but to master the currents of modern markets, and if you're poised to unlock the doors to financial sovereignty. No matter your previous successes or stumbles, our journey together is about moving forward, about turning intricate financial mechanisms into levers of prosperity.

Thank you for choosing this guide. I invite you now to dive in, to immerse yourself in the strategies and insights that lie ahead. Together, let's unlock the wealth that awaits.

Chapter 1: The Basics and Beyond: Mastering Basic and Advanced Investment Strategies

Amelia stood, her eyes locked onto the chessboard of high-finance that sprawled across the twin monitors on her mahogany desk. She was poised like a seasoned general before a campaign, weighing her next move in light-streaked solitude, morning rays casting long shadows in her spacious office. The soft hum of the city awakening filtered through the panoramic window, a testament to commerce and ambition. She drew in a breath, tasting the tension of a decision hanging in the balance.

Thomas, her business partner, broke the silence. "Options and debentures," he said with a quiet intensity that matched hers. "Either could be the linchpin in our approach, but we'll need a steady hand." He handed her the latest market analysis, his fingers brushing hers with a shared understanding of the risks ahead. As Amelia flipped through the pages, the scent of paper mingled with a medley of numbers and predictions, her mind danced to the rhythms of potential and peril that they spelled out in sobering clarity.

The chatter of advisors in a nearby conference room seeped through the walls—muffled voices grappling with similar quandaries. She could sense the undercurrent of hope and hesitance that threaded their discussions, a reflection of her own internal debate. Their collective apprehension sculpted the office air, as tangible as the stainless steel statue of Lady Fortune that watched over them, her scales tipped ever so slightly toward those who dared to venture beyond the ease of common stocks.

Her father's words, though spoken many years past, surged to the forefront: "Diversification isn't merely a strategy; it's an act of survival in a sea that shows no mercy to the unwary." Those words had cost him. He had been a man unmoored by an untamed market—talented, yes, but tethered to antiquated investing philosophies that became his downfall. Amelia's resolve hardened with the remembrance. She would not repeat his history; the options market with its convoluted promises and pitfalls offered a chance to transcend, to forge a new dynasty on the bedrock of adaptability.

Her gaze slipped beyond the immediacy of her office, to the city throbbing with life and commerce. There, in every building and every person, lay a story of choices, gambles, of success and failure. She felt an invisible thread that connected her to each of them, this kinship of risk and reward.

Could she harness the intricacies of options and convertible debentures, not as mere tools but as extensions of her vision—melding preservation with aggression, balancing boldness with the prudence of kings? Would she fashion a fortress in her portfolio that could withstand the inevitable sieges of market volatility? "To win, one has to play," she whispered to no one.

As she stood there, the light of dawn embraced her, illuminating the path of investors past and the uncharted routes that beckoned to her. In the stillness of the burgeoning day, her spirit soared on the wings of probability, a galvanizing mixture of fear and exhilaration.

Will Amelia's strategic choices lead her to the success that eluded her father, or will the complexities of advanced investment strategies prove to be a siren song, drawing her toward unforeseen reefs?

Elevate Your Wealth Beyond the Basics

The financial landscape today is a complex maze, riddled with opportunities that, if navigated correctly, can lead to unprecedented wealth accumulation. The key to unlocking this potential lies not just in grasping the fundamentals but in mastering the intricate dance of advanced investment strategies. This journey into sophisticated investment avenues is not just about amplifying assets; it's about crafting a portfolio so resilient, so diverse, that it not only withstands the market's capricious nature but thrives amidst it.

Understanding the stock market is the cornerstone of any successful investment strategy. It's essential, yes, but consider it merely your entry ticket to the grand arena of wealth creation. Here, option securities and convertible debentures emerge as potent tools in an investor's arsenal, offering strategic advantages that go well beyond the scope of traditional stocks and bonds. The crux of our discussion pivots on these instruments not because they're exotic or complex, but because their proper utilization aligns seamlessly with mitigating risks and maximizing returns — the very essence of investing.

In identifying **scenarios where sophisticated investment opportunities shine**, it becomes evident that the intricacies of these tools are not hurdles but bridges. Bridges that lead investors across turbulent waters, helping them harness volatility to their advantage. The beauty of these mechanisms lies in their ability to transform perceived market threats into lucrative opportunities, provided one knows when and how to deploy them.

Diversifying and fortifying your portfolio against market volatilities isn't just a defensive tactic; it's an assertive move towards wealth accumulation. Applying advanced investment strategies transforms your portfolio into a dynamic entity, capable of adapting and evolving in response to market changes. This adaptiveness is not rooted in mere speculation but in a deep understanding of market mechanisms and the strategic deployment of varied investment vehicles.

The overarching theme of our dialogue extends beyond these strategies. We delve into the realms of real estate, mutual funds, and the strategic nuances of tax planning — all critical components in the seasoned investor's toolkit. Each element is not standalone but interwoven, creating a tapestry of strategies that, when executed in concert, unveil a roadmap to financial freedom.

Addressing the **challenge many individuals face in navigating the complex financial landscape** to build substantial wealth, we dismantle the barriers of complexity and rapid inflation. By equipping you with the knowledge of innovative investment and tax strategies, this discussion serves as a beacon, guiding you through the fog of market intricacies towards your financial goals.

This narrative is not just a lesson; it's a dialogue with a trusted mentor. Through engaging insights and real-world applications, we endeavor to transform the theoretical into the tangible. By mastering these advanced strategies within the realm of investing and tactical tax planning, you stand on the threshold of financial freedom — a domain where your assets work not just for you, but because of you. The journey to unlocking your wealth potential begins with understanding the basics and beyond; it begins here, with the conviction that your financial aspirations are not just feasible but firmly within your grasp.

PART ONE: INTO THE WORLD OF STOCKS AND BEYOND

The stock market operates as the heart of the financial world, pumping wealth and opportunities through networks of investors and companies. At its core, it's a simple concept: buying shares in a company gives you a small ownership stake. However, to truly unlock the door to financial success, one must venture beyond this straightforward notion and explore the terrain of option securities and convertible debentures.

Imagine, if you will, a marketplace not unlike the vibrant bazaars of old, where merchants and buyers haggle over goods. In this bustling environment, options and convertible debentures are the exotic spices and rare fabrics. They offer nuanced flavors and distinctive qualities not found in the more straightforward purchases of stocks. Options provide the right, but not the obligation, to buy or sell a security at a predetermined price within a specified timeframe, offering a way to hedge against market fluctuations or speculate on future changes. Meanwhile, convertible debentures merge the safety net of bonds with the potential high returns of stocks, offering a convertible feature into shares at certain times during their lifespan.

Delving into the strategic advantages, one begins to appreciate the beauty of these instruments. Like a chess master contemplating a complex board, an investor can use options to take positions in the market with a predefined risk. These can be customized to fit various market outlooks, from bullish to bearish or even when expecting sideways movement. Convertible debentures, on the other hand, entice with their dual promise: the reliability of receiving interest payments with the upside potential of converting into equity should the company's stock perform well.

Yet, it's imperative to approach these sophisticated investment vehicles with a learner's mind. Grasping the fundamentals of how they work is akin to learning the language of a new country. It's the first step in a journey toward making informed decisions that align with one's investment goals and risk tolerance. Just as one wouldn't embark on a journey without a map, stepping into the realms of options and convertible debentures requires guidance and knowledge.

The essence of mastering the stock market lies not only in understanding its fundamental building blocks but also in embracing the sophisticated investment opportunities it presents.

PART TWO: MAXIMIZING RETURNS THROUGH SOPHISTICATION

In the pursuit of maximizing returns, the quest often leads beyond the beaten paths to terrains less traveled. Here lie sophisticated investment opportunities, akin to discovering hidden treasures that, when deployed judiciously, can significantly enhance the wealth of the astute investor. Identifying the scenarios in which these strategies shine brightest is akin to a navigator discerning the optimal route through treacherous waters.

Consider the market's cyclic nature – a series of ebbs and flows driven by underlying economic, political, and societal currents. In periods of volatility, options securities come into their own, offering a shield against the tempest while allowing the investor to capitalize on the tumult. Picture a surfer skillfully riding a wave. Options can be that surfboard, providing agility and protection as investors navigate the high seas of market unpredictability.

Convertible debentures serve their purpose too, especially in scenarios where the stock market is buoyant, and companies seek to raise capital without diluting equity prematurely. They are the bridge that connects the safe shores of fixed-income securities with the verdant, yet unpredictable, lands of equity investment. Like a seasoned trader crossing a bustling marketplace, investors wielding convertible debentures traverse the gap between risk and reward with a measured step, guided by the light of potential equity conversion.

The rhetorical question then arises: How does one discern the right time and the right situation to employ these sophisticated strategies? It is a matter of understanding the market's language, of listening to the whispers of trends and patterns, and of aligning one's investment strategies with both personal financial goals and the broader economic landscape.

Envisage a grand tapestry, where each thread represents a different investment opportunity. Sophisticated strategies like options and convertible debentures add depth and texture to this tapestry, enabling it to withstand the vagaries of time and circumstance. Through careful planning and strategic deployment, these instruments can clothe the investor in a garment of resilience and potential profitability.

How, then, can one weave these sophisticated threads into a personal investment portfolio that not only stands the test of time but flourishes?

PART THREE: THE ADVANCED INVESTOR'S COMPASS

A Descriptive Framework for Strategic Portfolio Enhancement (ASPECT)

Assessment Phase

At the outset, an investor must take stock of their current holdings, risk tolerance, and financial aspirations. This is much like a gardener assessing the soil and climate before planting. Understanding the composition of your portfolio and your comfort with risk sets the stage for all future decisions. Are you planted firmly in the soil of conservative investments, or are you seeking the more fertile ground of aggressive growth?

Planning Phase

With a clear view of one's investment landscape, the next step is to map out a strategy. This involves identifying opportunities that not only promise returns but align with your risk profile. Option securities and convertible debentures enter the scene here as potent tools. The choice of instrument is much like selecting crops based on the season's forecast; different conditions call for different approaches.

Implementation Phase

Next comes the seeding – the actual application of your strategy. This phase involves purchasing the identified securities, monitoring their performance, and adjusting positions as necessary. It's akin to a farmer tending to their fields, watchful of changes in the weather and ready to pivot strategies to protect their yield.

Review Phase

Finally, periodic evaluation of your portfolio's performance against your goals acts as the harvest of your efforts. It's a time to assess which strategies bore fruit and which did not, and to consider any adjustments needed as you prepare for the next planting season. This iterative process ensures your investment approach evolves in tandem with the market and your personal financial landscape.

Through the ASPECT framework, investors can navigate the complexities of the market with confidence. By carefully selecting advanced investment strategies that suit their risk tolerance and goals, they can diversify their portfolio and enhance its resilience against market volatilities.

Combining fundamental stock market understanding with sophisticated investment strategies like options securities and convertible debentures, and applying these insights through a structured framework, investors can effectively diversify and strengthen their portfolio against market fluctuations.

Embarking on the journey of mastering the art and science of investment, we begin by laying a solid foundation with **the basics of the stock market**. Here, we've dived deep into the world of option securities and convertible debentures, not merely as financial jargon, but as tools of empowerment towards building a robust investment portfolio. Recognizing these sophisticated investment opportunities as essential gears in the machinery of wealth accumulation, we open up a realm where strategic diversification becomes not just a possibility, but a practical reality.

Unlocking Sophisticated Investment Opportunities

The journey from understanding the fundamental elements of the stock market to identifying when and how to employ advanced investment strategies is akin to learning a new language. It is about *discovering new ways to express your financial goals and dreams*, taking the insights offered by options, convertible debentures, and other securities to articulate a narrative of growth and resilience. The essence here is not just in knowing these tools exist, but in acquiring the know-how to use them effectively to mitigate risks and maximize returns.

Diversify and Fortify

Imagine your investment portfolio as a ship navigating through the vast, unpredictable ocean of market volatilities. The advanced investment strategies discussed are the sails and rudders designed to keep you afloat and on course through both calm seas and tempests. It is about having a diversified set of tools at your disposal, each offering a unique advantage in bolstering your ship against the tides of economic shifts and uncertainties. By strategically diversifying your portfolio, you not only set yourself up for enduring success but also create buffers that safeguard your assets.

As we turn the page on this initial chapter, the pathway we've begun to tread is illuminated with possibilities. The insights provided are not mere stepping stones, but powerful catalysts for transformation. With each strategy discussed, we unlock doors to opportunities that have the potential to reshape not just portfolios, but lives.

The beauty of this journey lies in its ability to reward those who dare to venture beyond the familiar horizons of traditional investment avenues. It beckons you, the reader, to explore, to experiment, and to excel. Armed with the knowledge and strategies shared, the pathway to financial freedom is not just a dream envisioned in the distant future; it is a tangible goal that lies within your grasp in just 1 to 2 years.

Encouraged by the insights from this chapter, the road ahead promises to be an exciting exploration of further advanced mechanisms to amplify your assets. Each page turned is a step closer to unlocking the full potential of your financial future. Engage, educate, and empower yourself through this journey, and the rewards will be both enriching and enduring. Remember, the art of savvy investing and tactical tax planning, as we will continue to uncover, are your keys to unlocking **wealth unbounded**.

Chapter 2: Revolutionary Real Estate: Building Wealth Brick by Brick

The sun was on its westward descent, draping a golden blanket over the city as Jonathan closed the crisp folder labeled "Hamilton Estates Proposal." The leather chair he sat in served as a constant — the only item that journeyed with him through every office upgrade. At the horizon of his mind, dreams of a new development danced and wavered like the heat from the pavement below his corner office window.

He recalled the wisdom of his mentor, that real estate wasn't simply about brick and mortar; it was about the envisioning of a future, the structuring of finance, and the subtle art of negotiation. Jonathan knew that the path to wealth lay not in the land itself, but in the carefully woven strategies employed to acquire and harness it.

A laugh echoed from outside his office, shattering his concentration. His eyes momentarily joined the office hustle — the orchestrated ballet of brokers and clients, the fervent tapping of calculators. The scent of freshly brewed coffee wafted in, piquing his senses, reminding him of the endless hours he spent mastering the intricacies of amortization and interest rates. Determined, he dove back into the pool of his thoughts, piecing together his negotiation strategy to secure a mortgage with terms that would favor the empire he was meticulously building.

In the solitude of his office, Jonathan pondered the last piece of the puzzle — the protective cloak of an LLC. He mulled over the transactions of his past, where each property became a carefully placed chess piece, shielded by the anonymity and security that the corporate entity offered. Like a confidant, the LLC whispered promises of tax optimizations and liability containment; a boon to any investor looking to play in the high stakes game of portfolio development.

His fingers paused above the keyboard, hesitating as he contemplated the balance between risk and protection. In this dance of numbers and law, he grasped at the threads of a future not yet written. A phone call interrupted his reverie, a potential investor singing tunes of opportunities and partnerships. The music of possibility filled the room, and as he jotted down notes, a cartographer plotting the uncharted territories of tomorrow.

As the office lights dimmed and the echoes of daytime activity softened to a murmur, Jonathan stood, gazing upon the empire that sprawled beneath him, a tapestry of goals, dreams, and persistence. How many others, he wondered, stood at the threshold of their future, armed with knowledge and tactics, ready to weave their aspirations into the fabric of the city?

The Blueprint to Building Wealth Through Real Estate

Real estate investment stands as a cornerstone in the edifice of wealth building, offering both stability and tremendous growth potential. Yet, many aspiring investors find themselves at the starting line, overwhelmed by the complexity of terms, strategies, and regulations. The journey to unlocking wealth through real estate need not be labyrinthine. By honing in on **strategic real estate portfolio development,** one can navigate through the oft-overlooked intricacies of mortgage structuring, negotiation tactics, and the shrewd use of Limited Liability Companies (LLCs) to not just acquire property, but to lay the groundwork for long-term financial prosperity.

The endeavor begins with a deep dive into **mortgage structuring.** Understanding the framework of your financial commitments plays a pivotal role in real estate investment. From fixed-rate mortgages offering the stability of predictable payments to the potential short-term benefits of adjustable-rate mortgages, each type comes with its own set of advantages and trade-offs. Critical to this is mastering the art of negotiation — not merely as a skill but as an essential strategy for securing terms that tilt the balance in favor of your financial goals. Lower interest rates and longer loan terms can significantly reduce your outlays and enhance your investment's profitability.

Transitioning into the realm of **LLCs,** many investors discover a powerful vehicle for optimizing financial gains while safeguarding personal assets. The process of establishing an LLC for real estate ventures, though bureaucratic, offers a shield against personal liability and can provide tax advantages that are too significant to overlook. It's about structuring your investments in a way that maximizes protection and minimizes risk — a principle that underpins prudent wealth accumulation.

At the heart of a successful real estate venture lies a **comprehensive investment strategy.** It's not merely about possessing a portfolio of properties but understanding the market dynamics, conducting thorough due diligence, and evaluating the potential of every asset with a discerning eye. This step is where the theoretical converges with the practical; where market research, property analysis, and instinctual foresight coalesce to identify opportunities that promise both rental yield and capital appreciation.

The Pathway to Profit: A Structured Approach to Real Estate Mastery

Step 1: Understanding Mortgage Structuring

Begin with demystifying mortgages. Spend a week to grasp the nuances between fixed and adjustable-rate mortgages.

Evaluate which aligns with your financial objectives, factoring the market forecast into your decision-making. Develop negotiation strategies; this could mean refining your communication skills or understanding the lender's perspective. Aim for a measurable improvement in the terms you secure, such as a 0.5% reduction in interest rates or extending the loan term by five years.

Step 2: Leveraging LLCs for Real Estate Investments

Allocate a month to the nitty-gritty of setting up an LLC. Start by learning the benefits and then meticulously go through the process of registration, obtaining an EIN, and perhaps consulting a tax advisor to ensure you're optimizing your tax position. The goal is to have your LLC operational, ready to be the protective vessel for your real estate transactions.

Step 3: Comprehensive Approach to Real Estate Investment

Dedicate another month to mastering market research and property analysis. This isn't about a cursory glance at trends, but a deep dive into demographics, economic indicators, and local market peculiarities that can impact your investment. Your aim is to be able to pick out investment opportunities that others might overlook, with a clear understanding of the potential rental income and appreciation.

Step 4: Financing Options for Real Estate Investments

Spend two weeks exploring financing options. Beyond traditional mortgages, familiarize yourself with hard money loans, seller financing, and other creative financing strategies. Analyze how each can fit into your investment strategy, looking for those that provide the best terms and flexibility for your goals.

Step 5: Managing and Growing a Real Estate Portfolio

Over the following two months, focus on portfolio management. Learn the best practices for property management, tenant screening, and strategies to maximize rental yield. Simultaneously, study the market for expansion opportunities, whether through acquisitions or development projects, with a goal of increasing your portfolio's value and income potential by a specific target, say 20%.

This step-by-step process isn't just about accomplishing tasks; it's a transformational journey that imbues your investment philosophy with depth and resilience. By the end of it, not only will you have fleshed out a robust real estate portfolio, but you'll also possess the acumen to navigate the complex waters of real estate investment, ensuring sustainable growth and wealth accumulation.

Remember, the key to mastering real estate investment lies not in executing transactions but in crafting a strategy that respects the nuances of financial structures, utilizes legal entities for protection and advantage, and prioritizes long-term wealth over short-term gains. Through this disciplined approach, you'll unlock not just the door to immediate success in real estate but the pathway to enduring financial freedom.

Navigating the complex world of mortgages can feel like deciphering an ancient script. Yet, the ability to demystify this script is a vital first step toward securing a foundation for wealth through real estate investments. At its core, understanding mortgages is about recognizing that not all loans are created equal, and the right kind of loan can make a substantial difference in your financial health.

Fixed-rate mortgages offer the comfort of predictability, locking in an interest rate for the duration of the loan. This means your payments remain constant, shielding you from the ups and downs of market fluctuations. On the other hand, adjustable-rate mortgages (ARMs) might start with a lower interest rate, providing an attractive short-term option for those willing to bet on future market trends. However, this comes with the risk of interest rates climbing, potentially increasing monthly payments unpredictably.

Imagine walking into a negotiation with a lender armed with the knowledge of these mortgage types and their implications. It's somewhat akin to choosing between a steady, reliable workhorse or a swift, yet unpredictable racehorse. Each has its advantages, contingent on the journey ahead. Knowing when to leverage the stability of a fixed-rate versus the potential cost savings of an ARM can be crucial.

Securing favorable terms with lenders goes beyond simple interest rates. Understanding the nuances of mortgage terms, payment structures, and the potential for negotiation empowers investors to tailor their financing in a way that aligns with their long-term investment goals.

The Path to Leveraging LLCs in Real Estate

Creating a Limited Liability Company (LLC) for real estate investments is like constructing an invisible shield around your personal assets. It's not just about separation; it's a strategic move to optimize financial outcomes while mitigating risks. The essence of leveraging an LLC lies in its dual advantage of offering asset protection and potential tax benefits.

Step 1: Understanding Mortgage Structuring

Navigating the sea of mortgage options begins with distinguishing the ships from the boats – recognizing the difference between fixed-rate mortgages and ARMs. The stability of fixed-rate mortgages can be likened to a reliable vessel, steady against the unpredictable tides of interest rates. ARMs, contrastingly, offer an enticing initial journey with lower rates, akin to a swift boat that may encounter turbulent waters as interest rates fluctuate. Within these waters, negotiation becomes the compass, guiding investors towards favorable terms that best suit their voyage's length and risk tolerance.

Step 2: Leveraging LLCs for Real Estate Investments

Setting up an LLC might sound daunting, but it's essentially like charting a new course on a map. Filing the paperwork is the first step, marking your territory. Obtaining an Employer Identification Number (EIN) is akin to acquiring the right navigation tools. This setup, though seemingly intricate, paves the way toward utilizing the LLC as a vessel to carry your investments safely, keeping the storms of personal liability at bay.

Step 3: Comprehensive Approach to Real Estate Investment

Understanding the terrain of real estate investment is key. It's not merely about acquiring land or property; it's conducting thorough reconnaissance through market research and property analysis. This groundwork allows you to locate treasures - properties with high rental income potential and appreciation value, much like an explorer unearthing hidden gems.

Step 4: Financing Options for Real Estate Investments

The landscape of financing options is vast and varied. Traditional mortgages might be the well-trodden paths, but hard money loans and seller financing are less conventional routes that could lead to undiscovered opportunities. Each path offers its unique vistas and challenges, aligning differently with each investor's expedition goals.

Step 5: Managing and Growing a Real Estate Portfolio

The growth of a real estate portfolio is akin to cultivating a garden, where the proper care, maintenance, and timely decisions on when to sow and when to harvest are crucial. Focused management, from screening tenants to optimizing rental income, ensures that this garden not only blooms but thrives, potentially blossoming into a veritable forest of wealth.

Does contemplating the strategic placement of an LLC in your investment arsenal bring a new perspective on protecting and augmenting your assets?

In the realm of real estate investment, the journey towards accumulating long-term wealth is more akin to a marathon than a sprint. The road is long and often winding, adorned with opportunities cleverly disguised as challenges. It is the comprehensive understanding of mortgage structuring and favorable negotiation tactics, the strategic employment of LLCs, and the adoption of a well-rounded investment strategy that equips investors to not only participate in the marathon but to excel in it.

Navigating this journey requires an arsenal of knowledge, from recognizing the importance of selecting the right mortgage to the protective advantages of an LLC, and the foresight to manage and grow a portfolio. It's the synthesis of these elements that forges a path towards enduring wealth.

Investors armed with this knowledge are not just participating in the race; they are setting the pace.

A comprehensive approach to real estate investment, fortified by strategic mortgage negotiation and the savvy use of LLCs, embodies the foundation of long-term wealth accumulation.

As we've navigated the realms of mortgage intricacies, LLC advantages in real estate, and the pathway to substantial wealth accumulation, it's clear that mastering these elements is not just beneficial but essential. The landscape of real estate investment is intricate, with each decision casting ripples into your financial future. Understanding this, let's reflect on the foundational pillars that will cement your journey toward amplified asset accumulation.

Mastering Mortgage Structuring and Negotiation

The art of mortgage structuring and negotiation is akin to a conscientious chess game; every move is strategic, aiming for an advantageous position. The ability to secure favorable mortgage terms is not just a skill—it's a leverage point in your investment journey. **Lower interest rates and favorable terms** can significantly reduce your financial burden, allowing you to redirect funds into further investments or bolster your financial security. Remember, the difference in even a fraction of a percentage point on your mortgage can translate to thousands saved in the long run.

The Power of LLCs

Operating your real estate investments through LLCs is a game-changer. This approach not only **optimizes your financial gains** by affording tax advantages and operational flexibility but also crucially **protects your assets.** Think of an LLC as a protective moat around your castle of assets, keeping unforeseen legal challenges at bay. This is not just about safeguarding; it's about smart structuring for growth, imbued with the foresight of a seasoned investor.

Embracing a Comprehensive Investment Approach

Lastly, a comprehensive approach to real estate investment is your blueprint for **long-term wealth accumulation.** It's the meticulous molding of your portfolio, where each property is a carefully selected brick in your expanding empire. Diversification, market research, and future-focused strategies are your tools of trade. Remember, real estate investment is not just about acquiring assets; it's about nurturing and evolving a portfolio that stands resilient against market fluctuations, generating sustained wealth.

As you step forward from this chapter, armed with the knowledge of tactical mortgage negotiation, the strategic use of LLCs, and a holistic investment outlook, remember this: the journey to mastering real estate investment is ongoing. It requires patience, continuous learning, and an unwavering commitment to strategic planning. But with these principles as your foundation, you're not just building wealth; you're crafting a legacy.

Keep these insights at the forefront of your mind as you propel through your investment journey. The path to unlocking financial freedom through real estate is both challenging and rewarding. Each decision you make, informed by the strategic insights we've explored, edges you closer to your goal of financial autonomy.

Embrace the journey, and let these principles guide your steps. Together, they form a potent formula for not just navigating but mastering the world of real estate investment. Your ambition, fueled by informed decisions, is your greatest asset. Forge ahead with confidence, and let the bricks of knowledge lay the foundation for your financial future.

Chapter 3: The Art of Tactical Tax Planning: Keeping More of What You Earn

Dawn's light caressed the uneasy waters of San Francisco's Bay as Jonathan sat, poised at the mahogany desk that smelled faintly of lemon oil and diligence. His fingers danced lightly over the calculator, clicking in a soft staccato rhythm. The sharp tang of black coffee, mixed with the salt breeze, lingered on his palate. Tax season approached with the relentless certainty of the tides.

Across the room, an array of neatly stacked financial statements and tax reports sketched a landscape of his fiscal year. The documents told stories of judicious investments and bold entrepreneurial ventures. Yet beyond the steadied assurance of IRA contributions and the comfort of mortgage interest deductions, Jonathan knew the tale of his financial journey warranted a new chapter, one punctuated with strategic brilliance befitting his ambition.

He sifted through the dull hum of last year's strategies, recalling a seminar where whispers of tax optimization seeped into conversations, enticing as the sirens' call. They spoke of methods uncharted, hushed tones discussing real estate maneuvers, small business health reimbursement arrangements, and even trusts designed to transform the burden of tax into the boon of legacy.

His daughter's laugh, spilling in from the garden below, interrupted the chorus of fiscal thoughts. Her innocence reminded him why he sought to build an edifice of wealth not merely to possess but to bestow. With her future shimmering on the horizon, more resplendent than the sunrise before him, Jonathan desired not just to build wealth but to bear it forward, to plant seeds that would bloom long after his time.

The city was waking now, a creature stretching its limbs of bridges and streets, and as the clatter of the world outside grew louder, the room seemed too quiet just for him. The numbers on his screen were not just numbers; they were keys to a vault of possibility, each potential strategy a cast of light into shadows of uncertainty.

But which path to take? Could the indistinct outlines of advanced tax planning methods be the map to the treasure he sought, or were they merely mirages? With each calculation, Jonathan skirted closer to an answer, his resolve hardening like the rolling fog turning to mist, revealing the city's silhouette once hidden.

Could the insights of the few elevate the fortunes of the

diligent? What untold riches lie hidden behind the veil of complexity, waiting for those daring enough to delve into the arcane art of tax optimization?

Unlock Your Financial Potential with Tactical Tax Planning

Tax planning may not be the first thing that comes to mind when dreaming of wealth and financial freedom. Yet, it's a secret weapon in the arsenal of the financially astute. Beyond the basic tax-saving strategies known to most, lies a world of advanced, tactical tax planning that could significantly shift your financial landscape from steady growth to exponential expansion. In this pivotal chapter, we dive into the sophisticated world of tax planning, exploring the nuanced strategies that can help you keep more of what you earn and, more importantly, grow those earnings at an accelerated pace.

Many view taxes as a fixed, immutable drain on their resources, overlooking the dynamic strategies that can drastically reduce their taxable income. While charitable donations and 401(k) contributions are commendable for their simplicity and effectiveness, they represent just the beginning of what's possible. Specialized tax solutions tailored to specific financial situations are the key to unlocking additional income streams without increasing your tax liability. Through creative tax optimization, individuals can carve out more room for investment and growth, transforming tax planning from a defensive chore into a potent tool for wealth building.

The Blueprint to Tactical Tax Elevation

Step 1: Exploring Specialized Tax Solutions

The journey into tactical tax planning begins with an exploration of specialized solutions that go beyond the surface-level strategies. Tax credits, deductions, and exemptions tailored to your unique financial scenario can significantly lower your taxable income. For example, understanding and leveraging cost segregation can accelerate depreciation on certain aspects of real property, offering substantial tax savings. Similarly, tax-free exchanges under specific conditions allow for the deferral of capital gains taxes, preserving more of your capital for re-investment.

Step 2: Mastering Creative Tax Optimization Techniques

Next, we must master the art of creative tax optimization, designing a strategy that complements your personal financial goals. This involves more than just selecting the right investments; it requires a holistic approach to how your finances interact with tax laws. Strategies such as income shifting, investing in tax-efficient assets, and maximizing contributions to tax-advantaged accounts can all play a pivotal role. Through vivid examples and case studies, this step demonstrates the transformative power of these techniques in reducing your tax bill while enhancing your wealth.

Step 3: Implementing Advanced Tax Planning Methods

Implementing advanced tax planning strategies into your financial portfolio is crucial for sustained wealth-building. Techniques like tax loss harvesting can turn investment losses into opportunities for tax reduction, while strategic charitable giving and estate planning can protect your assets from excessive taxation, ensuring that you—and not the taxman—control the largest possible portion of your wealth. This step offers practical advice on integrating these methods into your financial planning, emphasizing the importance of a synergistic approach for maximum efficiency.

Step 4: Tracking and Monitoring Tax Savings

Finally, establishing a system to track and monitor your tax savings is vital. This not only allows you to see the tangible benefits of your strategic tax planning but also enables ongoing optimization. By providing tools and templates for effective record-keeping, this step ensures you can adjust your strategies in real-time, responding to new opportunities or changes in the tax code with agility.

This methodical approach to tactical tax planning is not just a theoretical exercise; it's a practical guide designed to be incorporated into your financial life. While the process may seem complex, the fundamental goal is clear: **maximize your wealth by minimizing your tax liability** through strategic, informed decision-making. By treating tax planning as a dynamic element of your financial strategy, you can unlock doors to growth that remain closed to those following a more passive approach.

By embracing the specialized, tailored strategies discussed in this chapter, you can transform the way you view and manage your taxes. No longer a mere obligation, tax planning becomes an integral component of your overarching strategy for financial freedom. Let this chapter serve as your handbook for navigating the intricate world of tactical tax planning, guiding you toward a future where you keep more of what you earn and multiply it with unparalleled efficiency.

Exploring beyond the familiar is not just a venture for the adventurous but a necessary quest in the realm of tax planning. Most are familiar with the usual tax-saving heroes: the charitable donations, the 401(k)s, and the IRAs. They're the trusty friends we lean on when April 15 looms. But the landscape of tax planning is vast and complex, filled with lesser-known strategies that can significantly reduce taxable income. Understanding these specialized tax solutions is akin to discovering hidden treasures that can bolster your financial arsenal.

Imagine for a moment that your income is a stream of water flowing into a vast ocean, with taxes representing the nets that catch much of this water before it reaches the ocean. The common tax strategies are like small holes in these nets, allowing some of the water to slip through—yet so much more water could reach the ocean if only the nets had more and larger holes. Specialized tax solutions create these larger holes, letting a greater volume of your income flow through to your personal financial ocean. From cost segregation studies that accelerate depreciation deductions on properties to tax-free exchanges allowing real estate investors to defer capital gains taxes, these strategies are the tools that create larger gaps in the tax nets.

Each of these specialized solutions is tailored to specific financial situations and goals. For example, a small business owner might leverage a Section 179 deduction to immediately expense the cost of qualifying business equipment, instead of depreciating those items over time. On the other hand, an investor might use a tax-loss harvesting strategy to offset realized capital gains with losses from other investments, thereby reducing taxable income. These strategies require a deeper understanding of tax laws and proactive planning, but the effort can lead to substantial savings.

Delving into these solutions starts with education and understanding. It's about making the commitment to explore the lesser-known parts of the tax code and seeking advice from knowledgeable professionals. With each new strategy uncovered, the potential to reduce taxable income grows, paving the way for substantial financial growth.

To capture the breadth of your income's potential, venturing beyond common tax strategies is essential.

Crafting a Tax-Savvy Blueprint

The journey toward mastering creative tax optimization techniques is both an art and a science, requiring a balance of knowledge, intuition, and strategic planning. The process begins with exploring specialized tax solutions, stepping beyond the comfort zone of standard deductions and into the realm of creative financial engineering.

Exploring Specialized Tax Solutions

The first step is akin to mapping the uncharted territories of the tax code, where treasures like tax credits, deductions, and exemptions await. For instance, understanding the nuances of cost segregation can be a game-changer for real estate owners, enabling them to accelerate depreciation on certain aspects of their properties. Alternatively, tax-free exchanges offer a pathway to defer capital gains taxes, providing breathing room to reinvest in new ventures.

Mastering Creative Tax Optimization Techniques

The next phase is where the canvas of your financial future is painted with broader strokes. Here, income-shifting strategies can be employed to distribute taxable income among family members in lower tax brackets. Tax-efficient investments, such as municipal bonds, offer returns that are exempt from federal (and possibly state) taxes, optimizing after-tax income. Utilizing tax-advantaged accounts like Roth IRAs or HSAs further enhances your portfolio's tax efficiency, all contributing to a more vibrant financial picture.

Implementing Advanced Tax Planning Methods

With a solid strategy in place, the focus shifts to weaving these individual techniques into the fabric of your overall financial portfolio. This might involve sophisticated methods like tax-loss harvesting to offset gains, or tax-efficient charitable giving through donor-advised funds. Estate planning then becomes a critical element, ensuring that your wealth serves your legacy in the most tax-advantaged manner possible.

Tracking and Monitoring Tax Savings

The final stroke on your masterpiece involves vigilance in tracking and monitoring the effectiveness of your tax-saving strategies. Utilizing tools and templates for record-keeping, alongside regular reviews with your tax professional, ensures that your strategies evolve in alignment with changing tax laws and personal financial situations.

How might adjusting your approach today reflect in the financial landscape of your tomorrow?

An Analytical Framework for Tactical Tax Planning: TAPIT

Analysis

The starting point of the TAPIT framework involves scrutinizing your financial landscape. This component is like laying out a puzzle, where each piece represents an element of your financial life—sources of income, potential tax liabilities, deductible expenses, and applicable credits. Recognizing these variables allows you to see the full picture and identify opportunities for optimization.

Strategy Formulation

In this phase, you weigh various tax planning strategies against each other, measuring their potential impact on your taxable income. It's akin to choosing your tools before sculpting a block of marble; each decision shapes the outcome. Whether it's deciding between maximizing 401(k) contributions or investing in tax-efficient mutual funds, this step is about crafting a tailored plan that aligns with your financial goals.

Implementation

Executing your tax planning strategies is much like planting a garden; it requires careful timing and compliance with tax laws to ensure that each strategy blooms to its full potential. Whether it's selling off losing investments at the right time for tax-loss harvesting or timing charitable donations to maximize deductions, proper implementation is key to reaping the benefits of your planning.

Monitoring

The final component involves regularly assessing the performance of your tax strategies, ensuring they adapt to both the changing landscape of tax law and your evolving financial situation. It's similar to tending a garden; constant care and adjustments ensure growth and vitality. Monitoring allows you to tweak or change strategies that are no longer as effective, maintaining the health of your financial portfolio.

Integrating tactical tax planning into your financial strategy unites the three pillars of tax efficiency, allowing for unparalleled growth and wealth accumulation.

As we wrap up our exploration into the art of tactical tax planning, it's clear that the journey toward amplifying one's assets requires a strategy that extends beyond the confines of conventional wisdom. The essence of truly transformative wealth building lies not only in how much you earn but significantly in how much of it you manage to keep. The narrative of financial growth is incomplete without a meticulous script on tax optimization.

Discover Specialized Tax Solutions

Tailored tax solutions are the unsung heroes in the narrative of wealth building. While the baseline practices give us a good start, diving deeper into customized strategies unveils a realm of possibilities that many overlook. Think of it as having a bespoke suit tailored; generic sizes can fit many, but a suit tailored to your exact measurements stands apart. Similarly, personalized tax strategies ensure that your financial plan isn't just good, but exceptional, fitted precisely to your unique financial contours.

Master Creative Tax Optimization Techniques

Embracing creativity in tax planning is not just about staying within the lanes legally, but about painting those lanes in the colors that best reflect your financial situation. It's about understanding that each stroke of optimization can brighten the canvas of your financial portfolio. For instance, employing tactics like tax loss harvesting or understanding the nuances of asset location can be akin to choosing the right shade in a masterpiece - it makes all the difference.

Implement Advanced Tax Planning Methods

The act of integrating advanced tax planning methods into your financial portfolio is essentially setting the sails correctly on your journey towards financial freedom. It's not enough to simply have these tools at your disposal; knowing when and how to deploy them can significantly alter the course of your wealth accumulation. Like a skilled sailor who reads the wind and waves to navigate, a savvy investor must read the financial landscape to build efficiency into their wealth-building efforts.

Tax planning is more than a mere obligation; it's an opportunity. An opportunity to leverage the rules of the game in your favor, to turn every possible stone and find the keys to a more prosperous future. *By stepping beyond the conventional pathways and choosing to delve into the specifics, you engage in a level of financial stewardship that sets you apart as a true architect of your wealth.*

Embrace these strategies with both confidence and caution, knowing that in the dynamic world of finance, staying informed, adaptable, and proactive is your best strategy. Let this knowledge empower you, but also remind you that the world of tax planning is ever-evolving. What stands as a peak strategy today may transform tomorrow. Hence, continue to educate yourself, consult with professionals, and never underestimate the power of tailored tax planning in your quest for financial freedom. Remember, every step you take in optimizing your taxes is a step closer to unlocking the full potential of your assets.

Chapter 4: The Accelerated Path: Proactive Investment for Quick Wins

In the animated fortitude of Manhattan's financial district, the sun filtered through the steel lattice of skyscrapers, casting geometric shadows on the pavement. Jasper Hawthorne stood pensively before the grand entrance of the towering edifice that housed the investment firm where he tailored fortunes. A wave of autumn wind nudged a flurry of documents from the hands of a flustered passerby, and Jasper helped gather the papers, his mind never far from the pursuit of fertile grounds in the tapestry of the market.

Inside his corner office, awash with the golden hue of a descending sun, Jasper's eyes darted between screens, charts whispering the secrets of industries in flux. Fragments of his own reflection mirrored back at him, a stoic mariner plotting courses through tempests of digits and decimals. His clients hungered for swift wealth accumulation, and Jasper, the artisan of assets, cast his net into the volatile sea with active management at the helm.

He contemplated the mosaic of his portfolio – technology start-ups ripe with innovation, real estate holdings anchored in regenerating districts, and health sector disruptors poised to redefine living. Diversification was not just strategy but a philosophical tapestry he wove from the threads of various investment vehicles, each unique in pattern, potential, and peril.

A trill from his phone pulled him from his reverie. A young couple prenticed under his financial guidance, zealous to build their fortune to purchase their dream home. Their voices were tinged with the glow of anticipation, and Jasper found himself the custodian of their aspirations, poised to morph dreams into tangible corners of the world.

As night replaced day, the office emptied, leaving behind a silence that hummed with the echo of trades settled and opportunities seized. Jasper stood by the window, the city's lights weaving constellations of commerce below. He mused over market trends, the pulse of geopolitical shifts, and nascent industries that promised swift financial growth. What new constellation of opportunities would the morrow unfurl in its ceaseless churn?

Might Jasper harness the unruly winds of fortune to steer his clients, and himself, closer to the shores of their desires?

The Need for Speed in Wealth Building

In the labyrinth of modern finance, actively managing your investments isn't just a good idea—it's a necessity for those yearning for rapid wealth growth. Gone are the days when a simple savings account could guarantee you a comfortable future. **In today's volatile markets, a proactive and diversified investment approach is essential.** It means being in the driver's seat of your financial journey, steering through the high-speed avenues of opportunity with precision and foresight.

Understanding the importance of active investment management for swift wealth accumulation is the first step towards unlocking financial success. It's about recognizing that passivity in the investment world equates to missed opportunities and diminished returns. Like a vigilant gardener, you must tend to your investments, pruning the underperformers and watering the potential winners, adapting strategies as the market landscape shifts. This active engagement not only mitigates risks but also positions you to capture growth as it happens.

Diversification is a term thrown around often, yet its true power is frequently underestimated. Evaluating a variety of investment vehicles is more than spreading your bets; it's about creating a resilient financial portfolio that can withstand market shocks while capturing upside potential across different sectors and geographies. Think of it as a mosaic, where each piece represents a unique asset class or investment strategy. Together, they form a comprehensive picture of financial stability and growth, tailored to meet your personal goals and risk tolerance.

Yet, this strategy requires a commitment to stay ahead with market trends, an often daunting task for the uninitiated. However, in the current financial climate, this proactive stance can be the difference between modest gains and significant financial leaps. It's about keeping your finger on the pulse, ready to pivot and capitalize on emerging opportunities. In a world where information is power, staying informed is not just advantageous—it's imperative.

The accelerating path to wealth doesn't mean recklessness. On the contrary, it demands a calculated approach, blending ambition with prudence. It involves balancing high-growth investments with stabilizing assets, ensuring that your portfolio is both dynamic and resilient. The goal is to outpace average market returns, and this can only be achieved by making well-informed, strategic decisions that are aligned with your financial aspirations and risk profile.

Imagine being able to streamline your path to financial freedom, compressing decades of slow, steady growth into just a few years of strategic, accelerated wealth accumulation. This vision is within reach, but it requires a departure from traditional investment paradigms. Embracing a mix of short-term gains with long-term investments, leveraging insights from market trends, and adjusting strategies in response to evolving economic landscapes are all part of the playbook for those looking to fast-track their financial progress.

To navigate this journey successfully, one must be both a student and a strategist—constantly learning, adapting, and applying new insights to refine their investment approach. The fruits of such labor are not just financial. They encompass the freedom to pursue passions, the peace of mind that comes with financial security, and the ability to leave a lasting legacy. **The accelerated path is not for the faint-hearted, but for the bold, the informed, and the proactive.** It's a journey that promises not just wealth, but a wealth of opportunities for those ready to embrace it.

Recognize the Importance of Active Investment Management for Swift Wealth Accumulation

Active investment management is at the heart of swift wealth accumulation. Unlike its passive counterpart, which involves holding investments for the long term with minimal trading, active management requires a hands-on approach. Investors must constantly evaluate their portfolios, make timely decisions, and leverage market trends to amplify returns. This strategy is pivotal for those who seek accelerated financial growth, as it capitalizes on short-term opportunities that passive strategies often overlook.

Imagine navigating a river in a kayak. Passive investment

might be likened to drifting with the current, a method that will eventually get you downstream, albeit slowly. Active investment management, however, is akin to paddling vigorously, steering deftly around rocks, and catching faster currents to reach your destination more quickly. This analogy underscores the essence of active investment: it's about making informed, proactive decisions to navigate the financial waters more deftly.

At its core, active investment management involves a deep dive into market research, financial forecasting, and strategic asset allocation. Investors must stay well-informed about market conditions, economic indicators, and potential growth sectors. By assessing these factors systematically, investors can position their portfolios to benefit from emerging trends and avoid downturns, thus outperforming their passive counterparts over time.

Yet, active management is not without its challenges. It demands time, knowledge, and an acute understanding of market dynamics. For many, this approach may seem daunting, yet the potential for accelerated wealth accumulation is significant. This strategy is especially beneficial in volatile markets, where the ability to adapt quickly can mean the difference between profit and loss.

The essence of accelerated wealth accumulation lies in the proactive, informed decisions of active investment management.

Evaluate a Variety of Investment Vehicles and How to Diversify Investments to Meet Individual Goals

Diversification is a cornerstone of sound investment strategy. It's the financial equivalent of not putting all your eggs in one basket. By spreading investments across various assets -- stocks, bonds, real estate, and more -- investors can mitigate risk and enhance the potential for returns. Each investment vehicle comes with its unique set of risks and opportunities, and understanding these is critical to building a robust investment portfolio.

Consider stocks, known for their potential for significant returns but also accompanied by volatility. Bonds offer more stability but typically yield lower returns. Real estate stands out for its potential for appreciation and rental income, albeit with higher entry costs and liquidity issues. Meanwhile, emerging assets like cryptocurrencies and commodities provide novel opportunities but carry their own risks. The trick lies in balancing these options to align with your personal financial goals and risk tolerance.

Think of diversification as crafting a meal. Just as you wouldn't want a meal comprised solely of desserts, in investing, relying on a single asset class can be equally unbalanced. A well-rounded investment "diet" includes a mix of assets, each serving a different role. Some provide growth potential, others stability, and some liquidity. The mix should cater to your financial goals, whether that's building wealth quickly, securing stable income, or preserving capital.

Creating a diversified portfolio involves more than just selecting a variety of assets. It requires a strategic approach: assessing each investment's performance potential, understanding how different assets interact with each other, and adjusting the mix over time. This tailored approach helps safeguard from market volatility and enhances the odds of achieving financial targets.

Yet, diversification doesn't eliminate risk altogether. It's about making informed choices to spread potential risks more broadly. Investors need to stay informed, periodically review their investment mix, and be willing to make adjustments in response to changing market conditions or personal circumstances.

Could understanding and leveraging the unique characteristics of various investment vehicles, combined with strategic diversification, be the key to unlocking your financial potential?

Stay Ahead with Market Trends to Capitalize on Fast Financial Growth Opportunities

Staying attuned to market trends is crucial for those aiming to accelerate their wealth growth. The investment landscape is ever-evolving, shaped by economic indicators, geopolitical events, and technological advancements. By keeping a finger on the pulse, investors can identify emerging opportunities and mitigate risks in a timely manner. This proactive approach is akin to a surfer who readies themselves to catch the next big wave—timing and knowledge are everything.

In the realm of investments, trends can manifest as shifts in consumer behavior, regulatory changes, or technological breakthroughs. For example, the rise of renewable energy sources has opened new investment avenues in green technology companies. Similarly, demographic shifts, such as an aging population, may indicate growing opportunities in healthcare and related sectors.

However, capitalizing on these trends requires more than mere observation. It necessitates a deep understanding of how these shifts can impact different industries and assets. Investors must analyze data, forecast potential outcomes, and discern whether a trend is a short-lived fad or the beginning of a long-term shift. This analytical process enables informed decision-making, allowing investors to adjust their strategies and seize growth opportunities as they arise.

Navigating market trends successfully also involves regular portfolio reviews. As the market landscape changes, so too should your investment mix. This dynamic approach ensures that your portfolio is aligned with the most promising opportunities while minimizing exposure to declining sectors.

Integrating proactive investment management, strategic diversification, and astute market trend analysis forms a comprehensive approach to accelerated wealth growth. This synergy enhances the potential for significant financial gains, providing a pathway to achieving financial freedom within a short time frame.

In this journey toward financial freedom, the road less traveled is often the one that leads to the greatest treasure. Embracing an active investment strategy is not just about making choices; it's about making informed choices. **Active investment management** is the cornerstone of rapid wealth accumulation, allowing you to navigate through the market's ebbs and flows with precision and agility.

Diversification: Your Financial Safety Net

Remember, diversification is not about putting all your eggs in different baskets haphazardly. It's about understanding which baskets are worth your trust and how many eggs you should place in each. By evaluating a variety of investment vehicles, you're not just investing; you're crafting a portfolio that reflects your goals, your risk tolerance, and your aspirations. It's akin to an artist choosing their palette before embarking on a masterpiece. Your financial portfolio, with its mix of stocks, bonds, real estate, and perhaps even cryptocurrencies, should be just that—a masterpiece reflecting your vision for the future.

Staying Ahead: The Pulse of the Market

Keeping your finger on the pulse of market trends is akin to a chef tasting their dish as it cooks. It's essential for making the necessary adjustments to achieve the perfect flavor—or in your case, the perfect balance of risk and reward. Staying informed allows you to seize fast financial growth opportunities, much like how a surfer catches the right wave to ride. It's not just about being in the water; it's about knowing when to paddle hard and stand up on your board.

By combining these elements—active management, diversification, and a keen eye on market trends—you're not just passively waiting for wealth to accumulate; you're actively chasing it down.

You have within your grasp the tools and insights needed to accelerate your path to financial freedom. Remember, wealth is not just about accumulating assets. It's about creating opportunities—for yourself, for your family, and for the generations that follow. Let this knowledge empower you as you move forward, making informed decisions that steer you closer to your financial goals.

Embrace this journey with confidence and curiosity, always willing to learn and adapt. The path to financial freedom is not linear; it is rich with twists and turns. But with a proactive and diversified investment approach, you're well equipped to navigate this complex landscape.

Let's move forward together, leveraging the power of informed investment decisions to unlock the wealth that lies ahead. Your financial future is bright, and the best time to start shaping it is now.

Chapter 5: After-Tax Returns: The Secret Sauce to Financial Gourmet

In the tepid glow of the fall afternoon, James sat on the weathered bench in Central Park, his mind chasing the tail of his finances like a dog in an endless game of cerebral fetch. His fingers traced the edge of an envelope that held his recent investment returns. As the rustle of leaves whispered tales of change, his brow furrowed under the weight of a dilemma, one that demanded he confront the erosion of his gains by the silent aggressor known as tax.

Across the footpath, children laughed, their joy unaffected by concerns of fiscal growth or government levies. James envied their innocence briefly before the ledger of his mind tallied once more the cost of neglecting to integrate tax planning into his financial strategy. The crisp air carried the scent of earthen decay and the unspoken promise of rebirth as he mulled over the past year's oversight.

He recalled his friend's advice, a chartered accountant who often spoke with animation about the judicious embrace of tax-efficient investing. The words came back to him now: "Save your profits from the taxman's reach as you would shield a flame from the wind." It was a striking visual, one that had him questioning if his reluctance to heed such counsel stemmed from ignorance or if it was a defiance born of the stubborn hope that hard work alone should suffice.

The city's hum faded into a distant murmur, becoming the backdrop to his contemplation. Growth within tax planning was not just an opportunity; it was a necessity, a crucial step in the dance of accumulation and preservation. James pondered the choices before him, growth stock mutual funds, retirement accounts, municipal bonds; each held the allure of potential shelter from the taxing storm.

A golden leaf, its edges tinged with the wisdom of autumn, landed quietly at his feet. It served as a metaphor for his financial future – even as it changed, it held the promise of new growth. If taxes were the winter of his contentment, then strategic tax planning could be the spring, fostering a rebirth of his fiscal affairs.

As the sun dropped lower, casting elongated shadows across the park, a distant bell tower chimed the hour, stirring James from his reverie. He stood, sliding the envelope into his coat pocket, and took a determined step forward. Tomorrow, he would seek counsel, forge a plan, and perhaps next year, he would be the one sharing insights on financial efficiency with friends.

Could it be that in the quest for wealth, the truest gains lie not just in the numbers that grace a bank statement, but in the strategic whispers that dance around them, unheard but ever-present?

Unlocking the Power of After-Tax Returns

Taxes are often overlooked in the pursuit of wealth accumulation, yet they play a pivotal role in the true realization of financial freedom. It's no secret that investors tirelessly seek avenues to amplify their assets, focusing intently on generating the highest possible returns. However, the sharp edge of tax implications can significantly slice away at those returns, leaving a much smaller piece of the pie than anticipated. This chapter delves into the sophisticated strategy of maximizing after-tax returns, an area where even experienced investors may find untapped potential.

The core principle here is **the impact of taxes on investment returns cannot be overstated.** Understanding this impact is paramount, as the difference between pre-tax and after-tax returns can be startling. The idea is not simply about earning more but about retaining more. By integrating strategic tax planning into your financial strategy, you're setting the stage for a more efficient and prosperous financial future.

Strategic tax planning isn't about finding loopholes; it's about knowing the rules of the game and using them to your advantage. It involves making investments in a manner that legally minimizes the amount of taxes owed, thus maximizing the amount of money that remains in your pocket. Every investment decision should be made with an eye towards its tax implications, considering factors like the tax rate on investment income, the timing of taxes, and the type of investment account.

One of the most enlightening insights you'll gain from this exploration is how **tax efficiency** can serve as a catalyst for opportunities for growth. By optimizing your after-tax returns, you not only preserve more of your wealth but also unlock the potential to reinvest those savings, further compounding your financial growth. This strategy can transform a seemingly modest return into a much more significant growth over time.

Yet, the art of tax-efficient investing requires a thorough understanding of the financial landscape. It is about making intentional choices with your investments that align with your overall financial goals, considering the tax implications of each asset class, and knowing when to hold, when to sell, and where to invest your assets. This is where the subtlety of strategic tax planning truly shines.

Ultimately, this chapter aims to equip you with the knowledge to **integrate strategic tax planning into your financial strategy,** transforming the way you view investment returns. It's about shifting your focus from merely generating high returns to optimizing after-tax returns. This subtle yet powerful shift is what can set the stage for a truly efficient and prosperous financial future.

In mastering the art of savvy investing and tactical tax planning, you're not just learning how to play the game; **you're learning how to play it well.** The key takeaway here is simple yet profound: by focusing on after-tax returns, you place yourself in a prime position to unlock new opportunities for growth, ensuring a smoother journey towards financial freedom. This is the secret sauce to financial gourmet, a vital ingredient in the recipe for amplifying your assets.

When it comes to investing, the impact of taxes can often be overlooked, but it plays a crucial role in the real returns you pocket. Imagine, if you will, planting a garden. You choose the seeds (investments) in hopes of growing a bountiful crop. However, part of your harvest has to be given up as a form of payment (taxes) for using the land. Just as the type of crop can determine the size of your dues, the kind of investments you make influences how much tax you will owe. Some investments are more "tax-efficient" than others, meaning they allow you to keep more of your returns after taxes.

Understanding the types of investments that are tax-efficient can significantly affect the after-tax returns of your portfolio. For example, municipal bonds might offer lower pre-tax returns than corporate bonds, but because the interest from most municipal bonds is exempt from federal income taxes (and possibly state and local taxes), they may actually provide a higher after-tax return depending on your tax bracket. This is why a keen awareness of tax implications on your investments is not just smart, but essential for maximizing your financial growth.

Moreover, employing strategies such as tax-loss harvesting, where you sell investments at a loss to offset the taxes on gains, can further optimize your after-tax returns. These strategies can be viewed as carefully pruning and weeding your garden to ensure the healthiest and most prosperous growth. By tactically reducing the tax impact, you ensure that more of your returns are working for you rather than being lost to taxes.

Yet, for many investors, the maze of tax laws and regulations can seem daunting. This is where seeking guidance from a tax professional or financial advisor can be invaluable. Just as a gardener might consult with a horticulturist to understand which plants are best suited for their soil, an investor needs to understand which investments are best suited for their financial situation and tax bracket.

In essence, incorporating tax-efficient investing into your financial strategy is pivotal for maximizing your portfolio's growth and ensuring that you keep more of what you earn.

Integrating Strategic Tax Planning

Strategic tax planning should not be an afterthought in your investment strategy; it should be a cornerstone. Imagine constructing a house. You wouldn't just focus on the exterior design without giving due thought to the foundational structure. Similarly, in your financial strategy, tax planning serves as the foundation that can support your efforts to build wealth.

Implementing tax strategies involves understanding not just the various tax-advantaged accounts available, such as IRAs and 401(k)s, but also how the timing of income and deductions can affect your tax liabilities. By selectively choosing when to recognize income or claim deductions, you can effectively lower your taxable income and, by extension, your tax bill. It's akin to choosing the right time to add essential nutrients to your plants to ensure they grow strong and healthy.

The real power of strategic tax planning lies in its ability to transform potential tax liabilities into opportunities for growth. For instance, by deferring taxes through the use of retirement accounts, you're essentially allowing your investments to compound over time tax-free, which can substantially increase your investment growth. This method showcases how strategic planning can turn a potential hindrance (taxes) into a powerful tool for wealth accumulation.

Furthermore, understanding the nuances of tax laws, such as how long-term capital gains are taxed differently from short-term gains, can lead to more informed decisions about when to buy or sell an asset. Each decision, much like deciding when to harvest a crop, can have significant impacts on your after-tax returns.

Yet, the effectiveness of any tax strategy depends on personalized circumstances—the fiscal soil, so to speak, in which your financial strategy is rooted. Therefore, a personalized approach, possibly with the help of a financial advisor, becomes paramount. They can help navigate the complexities of tax laws, much like a guide leading you through a dense forest, ensuring you can seize every opportunity to reduce tax liabilities and enhance your financial growth.

But how can you tailor tax planning to fit not just your current financial landscape but also prepare for future growth?

Uncovering Growth Opportunities Within Tax Planning

Recognizing opportunities for growth within tax planning involves a thoughtful analysis of your current financial situation and a forward-looking approach to future needs and goals. It's akin to cultivating a diverse garden that not only flourishes today but is also resilient and adaptable to changing seasons.

One key strategy involves the thoughtful allocation of investments across taxable and tax-advantaged accounts based on their tax efficiency. For instance, investments generating significant income or short-term capital gains, which are taxed at higher rates, can be placed in tax-deferred or tax-exempt accounts. This strategy ensures that the most tax-inefficient parts of your investment portfolio are sheltered from immediate taxation, allowing them to grow unimpeded by annual tax costs.

Another avenue for growth is the strategic conversion of traditional IRAs to Roth IRAs, known as a Roth conversion. This maneuver entails paying taxes on pre-tax assets now in anticipation of tax-free withdrawal benefits in retirement. Though this requires paying taxes upfront, the long-term benefits of tax-free growth and withdrawals can be substantial, especially if you expect to be in a higher tax bracket in retirement.

Moreover, understanding and leveraging tax credits and deductions can lead to substantial savings, which, if reinvested, can fuel further growth. Whether it's maximizing contributions to retirement accounts, taking advantage of educational tax credits, or employing charitable giving strategies, each decision can have profound effects on your overall financial efficiency and long-term wealth accumulation.

Tailoring these strategies to fit your unique financial landscape requires a nuanced understanding of both current tax laws and your personal financial goals. Like a gardener tweaking their strategy based on the climate, soil conditions, and types of plants they're cultivating, you must adapt your tax planning strategy to fit your specific financial ecosystem.

By integrating strategic tax planning into your financial

strategy and uncovering opportunities within tax planning, you position yourself to enhance financial efficiency and unlock new avenues for growth. Isn't it time to consider how a calculated approach to taxes can serve as the secret sauce in your recipe for financial success?

In the world of finance, understanding the nuanced dance between investments and taxes is more than just beneficial—it's essential. Embracing tax-efficient investing practices isn't merely a tactic for the financially elite; it's a game changer for anyone looking to secure a more prosperous future. By weaving strategic tax planning into the very fabric of your financial strategy, you open doors to optimized after-tax returns that can dramatically reshape your wealth accumulation over time.

The Zenith of Strategic Planning

One of the most compelling takeaways from our exploration is the undeniable impact of taxes on investment returns. Many investors, whether seasoned or novices, often splurge considerable energy chasing high returns without weighing the heavy anchor taxes can place on their gains. It's akin to running a race but ignoring the weight tied to your ankles. By integrating tax considerations into your investment decisions, you can not only lighten that load but also sprint towards your financial goals with greater ease.

The integration of strategic tax planning and financial strategy is more than just a good idea—it's a critical movement towards realizing your dream of financial freedom. Imagine planting a garden where each seed represents a different aspect of your financial strategy. Without the right soil, sunlight, and water—symbolizing thoughtful tax planning—those seeds may sprout but will never reach their full potential. Strategic tax planning ensures that your financial garden thrives, maximizing growth and yield.

Unlocking Paths to Growth

Discovering opportunities for growth within tax planning is akin to uncovering hidden treasures within your financial landscape. It's about seeking out roads less traveled, uncovering strategies that can propel your investments to new heights. This proactive approach not only enhances your financial future's efficiency but lays a robust foundation for wealth that can withstand the ebbs and flows of markets and tax laws alike.

It's imperative to remember that strategic tax planning is not a set-and-forget strategy. It requires continuous adaptation and recalibration in response to evolving tax laws, market conditions, and personal financial goals. By staying engaged and informed, you ensure that your financial strategy remains aligned with your objectives, adaptable to change, and always operating at peak efficiency.

As we pivot from this chapter to the next, bear in mind the

profound value of incorporating meticulous tax planning into your overall financial strategy. This holistic approach promises not just improved after-tax returns but a journey toward financial freedom marked by wisdom, strategic foresight, and an unyielding commitment to maximizing your assets. Let's carry forward the insights garnered here, wielding them as both shield and sword in the quest for financial excellence. After all, in the grand tapestry of wealth accumulation, being tax-savvy is not just an advantage—it's an absolute necessity.

Chapter 6: Customized Investment Strategies: Aligning With Your Risk Profile

Martha perched herself at the edge of her bed, the loosely knit afghan beneath her formed gentle creases where her fingers clutched. The morning light fluttered through the linen curtains, casting faint shadows on the wooden floor of her bedroom. Outside, the steadfast oak in her garden began to don green, whispering of the spring's return. Her garden was like her retirement account—an existence tended with patience and hope. But now there was a decision to weigh, heavy as the heirloom watch that lay cold on her nightstand.

She delved into the well of her mind, where thoughts of investment strategies swirled like leaves in a soft breeze. Conservative? It danced gracefully and predictably like the methodical ticking of her grandfather clock. But there was also the thrill of aggressive, like storms that sometimes brushed past her hometown—unexpected gusts promising invigorating rain but often leaving behind floods of regret.

Her neighbor Joe, ever the optimist, plunged his life savings into the latest tech frenzy. His demeanor shone with the intensity of his gamble, as if mirroring the screens that flashed numbers more volatile than the weather vane on his rooftop. He spoke with the fervor of prophets, but the circles under his eyes betrayed nights where peace was as elusive as the northern star in overcast skies. Could she risk such unrest?

Then there was Sue, a widow from two streets over, who toasted to the virtue of bonds and blue-chips. Her confidence came not from the promise of colossal gains, but from nights unhaunted by loss. Security swaddled her future like the comforting layers of a well-worn quilt.

Martha's fingertips grazed the surface of her mother's pearl necklace, tucked safely in an ivory box. Capital; wasn't it meant to grow yet remain unbroken? Like these pearls, a symbol of preservation, yet reflecting the ambition of light in their unassuming luster. The balance seemed as elusive as it was essential.

A burst of laughter rippled through the silence as children made their carefree way to the nearby school. Their ease left an echo in the room, tracing paths of what was and what could be. Will the seeds of risk bloom into a garden of prosperity or wither in an unexpected frost? The question lingered, as much in the heart as it did in the mind. How does one navigate the delicate equilibrium between guarding a lifetime's harvest and sowing for a more bountiful future?

Crafting Your Investment Masterpiece

Investing isn't just about putting your money into stocks and hoping for the best. It's an art form, requiring a nuanced understanding of your own risk tolerance, financial goals, and the broader market landscape. A misalignment in any of these areas can be the difference between thriving and merely surviving in the investment world. This chapter aims to shine a light on how to evaluate different investment perspectives—from the conservative savers to the aggressive investors—and align them with your unique financial canvas.

Understanding the Spectrum of Investment Strategies is the cornerstone of building a portfolio that not only grows but also aligns perfectly with your financial outlook. Many investors jump into the markets with an idea of what they want to achieve but without fully understanding where they stand on the risk tolerance scale. This is akin to setting sail without a compass; you might move forward, but the chances of reaching your desired destination are slim. By evaluating the different perspectives available, from the safety-first approach to the high-reward-high-risk strategy, you can begin to see where your comfort zone lies.

Creating a **Diversified Investment Plan** is the next step on this journey. Diversification isn't just a buzzword; it's a strategic approach to minimizing risk and maximizing returns. Think of it as not putting all your eggs in one basket—but with a twist. It's not just about spreading your investments across different assets but doing so in a way that reflects your risk profile and financial goals. Whether your focus is on capital preservation or aggressive growth, understanding how to weave together a mix of asset classes can make all the difference in achieving your objectives.

The balance between **Preserving Capital and Maximizing Returns** is perhaps one of the most critical aspects to understand when customizing your investment strategy. This balancing act is not static; it requires constant recalibration based on market conditions, life changes, and shifts in your financial goals. It's about finding that sweet spot where you're not losing sleep over market volatility but also not missing out on growth opportunities. This delicate equilibrium is where your investment strategy can truly flourish, tailored perfectly to suit your financial landscape.

The Path to Mastery

Investing, at its core, is a personal journey. It's about understanding yourself just as much as understanding the markets. By taking the time to evaluate your risk tolerance and financial goals, you can develop an investment strategy that not just works, but works for you. This strategy becomes your roadmap, guiding you through market fluctuations and life's unforeseen twists with confidence.

The real value lies in recognizing that this isn't a one-size-fits-all scenario. **Your investment journey is unique**. And while the principles of diversification and the balance of risk and return are universal, how they play out in your investment story will be distinctively yours.

In navigating this path, remember that the ultimate goal is not just financial gain but financial harmony. The right investment strategy aligns with your life's goals, not just your financial targets. It resonates with your risk tolerance, offering peace of mind alongside the potential for growth. This is the essence of crafting a customized investment strategy. It's not just about amplifying your assets but doing so in a way that amplifies your life's goals and dreams.

Embark on this journey with an open mind and a clear vision. The road to mastering your investment universe is filled with lessons and discoveries, each step tailored to align perfectly with your financial blueprint. Engage with this process, and watch as your portfolio—and your understanding of it—transforms into a masterpiece of personal and financial alignment.

Evaluating different investment perspectives is akin to choosing the best outfit for the weather; neither too hot nor too cold but just right for the conditions. Conservative investment strategies are like wearing a heavy coat in anticipation of a snowstorm – they aim to protect against the cold financial downturns, preserving capital at the cost of potentially missing out on the warmer, sunnier days of high market returns. On the flip side, aggressive strategies dive headfirst into the sunshine, wearing shorts and a t-shirt, aiming to soak up every ray of profit, fully accepting the risk of an unexpected chill.

While conservative investors might sleep easier at night, knowing their portfolio is wrapped in the warm layers of bonds and dividend-paying stocks, aggressive investors thrive on the adrenaline of the stock market's variability, cherishing the highs and weathering the lows. This dichotomy highlights the personal nature of investing – what feels too hot for one might be too cold for another.

To find your 'just right', it's crucial to assess not just your financial goals but also your emotional response to risk. Imagine if Goldilocks had a portfolio; her strategy would not be too conservative to stifle growth, nor too aggressive to risk it all. She'd find the perfect mix that lets her sleep soundly, knowing her investments are working for her at a risk level she's comfortable with.

The key to personal alignment in investing lies in understanding that there's no one-size-fits-all strategy. Each investor's mix of stocks, bonds, and other asset classes should reflect their individual goals, time horizon, and, most importantly, their comfort with risk.

By critically evaluating the range from conservative to aggressive investment perspectives, individuals can tailor their strategies to align perfectly with their financial objectives and risk tolerance.

Develop a Diversified Investment Plan

Crafting a diversified investment plan requires more than just a smorgasbord of assets. It's about finding the right ingredients that not only taste good on their own but also work together harmoniously – like the perfect culinary masterpiece. The goal is not to eliminate risk but to understand and manage it, blending the bold flavors of high-risk investments with the subtler tastes of safer assets to create a balanced portfolio.

An investor's ability to bear risk and sleep peacefully at night sets the stage for constructing a portfolio. It's like allocating your plate at a buffet. If you're someone who's squeamish at the sight of unfamiliar cuisine (high risk), then you might fill your plate with more familiar, comforting dishes (low-risk investments). Yet, a complete aversion to risk might mean missing out on discovering a new favorite (potential high returns).

To avoid such regrets, diversification employs a strategy that involves spreading investments across various asset classes to achieve a balance that respects both personal risk tolerances and financial objectives. Think of it as an insurance policy against your culinary curiosity gone wrong; if one dish doesn't sit well, you have many others to enjoy.

An analogy could be seen in assembling a music festival lineup. You want a mix of genres (asset classes) that cater to different tastes but together promise a memorable experience for everyone. Just as a festival would falter with a lineup that's too niche or too mainstream, an investment portfolio skewed too conservative or too aggressive may not reach its full potential.

One essential tool in this endeavor is the risk-reward ratio, determining how much risk to take for the expected return. It's akin to evaluating whether trying that exotic, spicy dish is worth the potential discomfort later – some may find the thrill and flavor worth the risk, while others prefer to stick to what they know and love.

As diversification is an art as much as a science, personal preference plays a crucial role in finding the balance that's just right. Moving beyond a one-size-fits-all approach allows for a nuanced strategy that accommodates personal risk tolerance while striving toward financial objectives.

Could understanding and embracing your unique risk appetite be the key to not just surviving, but thriving in the financial markets?

Understanding the Balancing Act

The art of balancing capital preservation with maximizing returns is akin to walking a tightrope. On one side, you have the safety net of capital preservation, ensuring that your hard-earned money does not meet an untimely demise. On the other, the allure of maximizing returns beckons, tempting you with the heights of potential gains. This act requires not just courage but a keen sense of balance and understanding of one's capabilities and limits.

In the realm of investment, capital preservation prioritizes safeguarding the principal amount over pursuing high returns. It's like opting for a sturdy, reliable car that gets you from point A to point B safely, if not spectacularly. Meanwhile, maximizing returns is about turbocharging that car, aiming for maximum speed but with increased risk of a crash.

Understanding this balance is crucial because it influences every investment decision, from the asset classes chosen to the individual securities within those classes. It entails recognizing when to be bold and when to be cautious, similar to knowing when to accelerate on an open highway and when to slow down in challenging conditions.

A balanced portfolio acts much like a well-trained tightrope walker, equipped with a long balancing pole—investments are spread across asset classes to stabilize the portfolio against market volatility. The weights of these investments can be adjusted, much like the tightrope walker shifts their pole, to maintain balance amidst changing economic conditions.

In practice, this balancing act is dynamic, not a set-and-forget strategy. Regular reviews and rebalancing are essential to ensure the portfolio remains aligned with the individual's risk profile and financial goals. It's akin to the tightrope walker's constant, subtle adjustments to maintain equilibrium.

Understanding the delicate balance between capital preservation and maximizing returns is vital for aligning investment strategies with one's risk profile and financial goals, ultimately crafting a diversified portfolio suited to individual needs.

Navigating the investment landscape can be as daunting as it is thrilling; understanding your risk profile is akin to selecting the right equipment before embarking on a grand adventure. What we've unpacked together in these pages is more than just a guide—it's a blueprint for aligning your financial aspirations with a strategy that resonates with your personal comfort level and goals.

Evaluate and Align

The heart of intelligent investing lies in knowing oneself. Your risk tolerance isn't just a static measure; it's a reflection of your financial situation, your goals, and, importantly, your emotional response to market fluctuations. By evaluating different investment perspectives, from the steadfast conservative to the boldly aggressive, you can pinpoint where you stand on this spectrum. It's akin to selecting the right gear for your journey; not everyone needs to scale the highest peaks to reach their destination.

Diversify and Plan

Diversification isn't just a buzzword; it's your financial safeguard. A diversified investment plan is your best defense against the market's unpredictability. Remember, it's not about eliminating risk—that's an impossibility. Instead, it's about **strategically managing risk** to cope with market volatilities without derailing your financial goals. Think of it as preparing for a variety of weather conditions on a trip; you may not use every piece of gear you pack, but you'll be glad to have options when the weather turns.

Balance and Optimize

The art of balancing capital preservation with maximizing returns is much like walking a tightrope; leaning too much on either side can lead to undesired outcomes. Preservation of capital ensures that you have a safety net, but being overly cautious can stifle growth. Conversely, an aggressive pursuit of maximization can expose you to unnecessary risk. The key is finding that sweet spot where your investments can grow at a pace that matches your risk tolerance and financial objectives.

Understanding your unique financial landscape and leveraging it to craft an investment strategy that reflects your goals and risk profile is not just wise; it's imperative. This process is ongoing and dynamic, adjusting as your life and the markets evolve. Armed with a deep understanding of your investment persona, a diversified plan, and a balanced approach to risk management, you are well-equipped to navigate the complexities of the investment world.

As we continue on this journey together, remember that investing is not just about the numbers; it's about creating a future that aligns with your vision of success. **By staying informed, adaptable, and aligned with your foundational principles, you unlock the potential to not just grow your wealth, but to forge a path toward financial freedom that is uniquely yours.**

The insights we've shared here are but stepping stones. As you delve deeper into the realms of savvy investing and tactical tax planning, keep these principles as your guide. Let them serve as a reminder that, in the realm of investing, knowledge, and alignment with one's self are the most powerful tools at your disposal.

Chapter 7: The Power of Diversification: A Safety Net Across Asset Classes

In the bleached twilight of an early spring evening, Michael stood before the wide window of his modest study, eyes tracing the silhouettes of the waking city. A soothing breeze, filled with the scent of blossoming trees, whispered through the slightly ajar window, carrying fragments of laughter and distant car horns. He turned back to the room, its walls lined with bookshelves burdened with wisdom of the ages, contracts, and market analyses. The room felt too still, suffocated by the weight of decisions lingering in the air like stale smoke.

He picked his way through financial spreadsheets strewn across the wide oak desk, fingers brushing the pie charts and graphs as if their textures held the secrets of the future. In his chest a knot of unease twisted tighter with each percentage point and market projection. He had spent years building his investment portfolio, a mosaic of stocks, bonds, and real estate, each a carefully placed tile in the grand scheme of his financial security.

The day had worn long with the news of market fluctuations

biting into his thoughts. He had weathered storms before, yet the bristle of volatility scratched at him anew. Michael had learned the hard lessons of an overzealous past, when the lure of high yields led to harsh awakenings and the cold comfort of hard truths. Each tick downward was a ghost from those days, a specter pulling him back to a time when risk mitigation and diversification were foreign concepts to his younger, more daring self.

A photo on the desk caught his eye, an echo of a sun-drenched afternoon in Santorini where the sea mirrored azure skies. A reminder of the dreams he harbored, each a ship seeking the far shore of a comfortable retirement, the freedom to pursue long-silenced passions of art and philanthropy, the desire to leave a legacy. But ships need safe harbors, and these aspirations drifted on the turbulent sea of market uncertainty. He recalled the advice of an old mentor who said, "Invest as if each dollar were a soldier in your army, sending them to different battles so that if one falls, another may rise."

The steady click of a clock broke the quietude, urging him to the present, to action. The air grew cooler, the breeze stronger, as if the world itself was drawing a deep breath before plunging into the unknown night. Tonight he would reshape his strategy, craft a bulwark against the tides with bonds, expand into new frontiers of commodities, and perhaps even delve into the nascent realm of digital currencies. His portfolio would become an atlas of exploration, each investment a marked location of calculated consideration and hope.

He slid into the high-backed chair, a knowing smile playing on his lips. He felt the fear dissipate, replaced by the warm glow of resolve. The path was set, the die cast, and unto the breach, he would go once more. Yet within his plan, a question lingered—would the careful spread of his resources weave the safety net his future required, or was there an unseen thread that needed tugging to unravel the best laid plans?

Unveiling the Veil: Mastering Asset Diversification

In a world teeming with investment opportunities yet flush with risks, crafting a resilient pathway to wealth accumulation requires more than just a whimsical selection of stocks or assets. **The power of diversification,** a cornerstone strategy for long-term wealth generation, stands as a testament to the adage "don't put all your eggs in one basket." This chapter invites you on an insightful journey to explore how diversifying across various asset classes not only mitigates risk but also maximizes potential returns. It's an exploration that reframes the concept of investment, transforming it from a gamble into a calculated strategy for financial victory.

The art of diversification extends beyond mere investment scattering. **It's about creating a safety net** that cushions against market volatility while ensuring your portfolio remains on course towards its ultimate destination: financial freedom.

Imagine navigating through the treacherous seas of the market with a vessel designed not only to withstand the storms but to leverage them for forward momentum. That's the essence of a diversified investment approach, a blueprint for sailing towards the horizon of wealth accumulation with confidence and poise.

Step 1: Fundamental Insights into Asset Class Navigation

Understanding the **fundamentals of investing across various asset classes** is akin to learning the language of the financial markets. Each asset class, be it stocks, bonds, real estate, or commodities, speaks with its own accent of risk and return. The melody of these accents, when harmonized effectively, composes a portfolio that reduces risk through diversification while striving for commendable returns. By anchoring your investment philosophy on this bedrock of understanding, you're better equipped to interpret the market's signals and make informed decisions that align with your financial goals.

Step 2: The Diversification Blueprint

Implementing effective diversification strategies is more than an act of balance; it's a dynamic process of continuously aligning your investment portfolio with your evolving risk tolerance and financial objectives. Here, we delve into the significance of asset allocation, not merely across asset classes but nuanced within each class by investment style, geographic region, and industry sector. It's about crafting a multifaceted investment portfolio that's robust in the face of market uncertainties, a testament to the strategic foresight that divides the seasoned investors from the novices.

Step 3: Steering Through Volatility

The hallmark of a well-diversified investment approach is its **capacity to navigate market volatility** with grace. In this segment, we explore the twin pillars of rebalancing and staying informed. Rebalancing ensures your portfolio does not drift too far from its intended risk profile, while staying updated on market trends allows for informed adjustments to your investment strategy. This dual approach empowers you to steer through the ebb and flow of market dynamics, maintaining course towards your financial goals with resilience and adaptability.

Step 4: The Art of Investment Selection

Finally, we broach the critical phase of **evaluating and selecting investment options.** This step is where theory meets practice, demanding a keen eye for details such as historical performance, risk metrics, and management track record. Equipped with the right tools and resources, you can conduct thorough investment research and due diligence, laying the groundwork for decisions that not only align with your financial objectives but also position you favorably within the risk-return spectrum.

By unfolding these steps with clarity and conviction, we embark on a transformative journey towards mastering the nuances of diversification. It's a strategy that not only enhances the quality of your investment portfolio but also imbues your path to financial freedom with a sense of security and optimism. Remember, in the realm of investments, diversity is not just a strategy—it's your safeguard against the unknown, your beacon guiding through the tumultuous seas of market volatility towards the shores of wealth accumulation and beyond. Embrace it.

Mastering the Fundamentals of Investment Diversification

At the heart of savvy investing lies an understanding that not all investments behave the same way at the same time. Stocks, bonds, real estate, and commodities each march to their own beat. By spreading your investments across these various asset classes, you effectively create a financial safety net, cushioning the blow should one part of the market take a hit.

Imagine you're at a buffet with a plate in hand. If you fill your plate with only one type of food and find out it's not to your taste, your entire meal is ruined. But if you diversify your choices, you're likely to enjoy your meal more because you're not dependent on one dish for satisfaction. This is essentially what diversification in investing aims to achieve – a satisfying financial 'meal' that isn't ruined by the underperformance of one 'dish'.

The benefits of investment diversification are manifold. By investing across different asset classes, you reduce the risk of a significant loss since not all asset classes will underperform simultaneously. This approach not only mitigates risk but can also smooth out the volatility of your investment returns over time. With a well-diversified portfolio, the impact of a poor performing investment is lessened by the stable or strong performance of others.

Yet, diversification is not a guarantee against loss. It's a strategy for managing risk more effectively. The goal is not to make quick gains but to build a stable foundation for long-term wealth generation. By understanding the unique characteristics and risk profiles of different asset classes, investors can make informed decisions on where to allocate their resources to maximize potential returns while managing their risk exposure.

Diversification across various asset classes is fundamental to mitigating risk and ensuring a stable foundation for long-term wealth generation.

The Diversification Navigator: Your

Guide to Building a Robust Investment Portfolio

Understanding the Fundamentals of Investing Across Asset Classes

When embarking on the journey of diversification, it's crucial to start with a solid understanding of the different asset classes. Stocks bring equity ownership in companies, attracting investors with the potential for high returns but also carrying significant risk. Bonds, on the other hand, offer a more stable investment, essentially lending money in exchange for periodic interest payments, but with lower return potential. Real estate provides tangible assets, offering both rental income and the possibility of appreciation. Commodities, including precious metals and oil, offer a hedge against inflation but can be volatile.

The beauty of diversifying across these asset classes lies in their distinct reactions to economic conditions. When stocks plunge due to market turbulence, bonds often remain stable or even increase in value, offering a buffer against loss. Real estate and commodities can serve as a hedge against inflation, preserving purchasing power when traditional financial instruments might falter.

To illustrate, consider the tech bubble of the early 2000s.

Investors heavily concentrated in technology stocks suffered significant losses when the bubble burst. In contrast, those with diversified portfolios, including bonds and real estate, experienced less volatility and preserved more of their wealth.

Implementing Effective Diversification Strategies

The next step is to implement your diversification strategy actively. This involves allocating your investments not just across different asset classes but also within each class. It's about spreading your eggs across multiple baskets and then ensuring each basket has a variety of eggs.

For stocks, this might involve diversifying across different sectors such as technology, healthcare, and consumer goods, and including a mix of large-cap and small-cap stocks. For bonds, consider a range of government and corporate bonds with varying maturities. In real estate, diversify geographically and across types of property.

One practical tip is to leverage index funds and ETFs (Exchange-Traded Funds) to achieve diversification efficiently. These funds pool together investments in a wide array of assets, offering instant diversification with a single purchase.

Navigating Market Volatility with a Diversified Approach

A diversified investment strategy is your best defense against market volatility. It allows you to navigate the ups and downs of the market with more stability, avoiding the roller-coaster ride that can come with a concentrated portfolio.

Regular portfolio rebalancing is critical to maintaining your desired level of diversification. This involves periodically adjusting your portfolio to keep your asset allocation in line with your risk tolerance and investment goals. When one asset class outperforms another, it can become a larger portion of your portfolio than intended, increasing your risk. By rebalancing, you sell some of what has increased in value and buy more of what has decreased, maintaining your diversification level.

Evaluating and Selecting Investment Options

The final step in building a diversified portfolio is selecting the specific investments within each asset class. This requires evaluating potential investments based on their risk, return, and how they fit into your overall portfolio.

Consider factors like historical performance, risk metrics, and the management track record. Utilize resources and tools available for investment research and due diligence to make informed decisions. Remember, the goal is not to pick the next big winner but to select investments that, when combined, create a balanced, diversified portfolio that aligns with your financial goals.

Could this approach be the key to unlocking a more stable and potentially more lucrative investing future?

The Portfolio Resilience Framework (PRF)

The Portfolio Resilience Framework (PRF) is a structured approach designed to guide investors through the process of creating a diversified investment portfolio that can withstand market fluctuations and support long-term financial goals.

Goal Setting

The first step in the PRF is to define your financial objectives and risk tolerance. Whether you're saving for retirement, a large purchase, or generating income, your goals will dictate your investment strategy. Knowing your risk tolerance helps to determine how much volatility you're willing to accept in pursuit of your financial objectives.

Asset Allocation

Based on your goals and risk tolerance, the next step is to decide on the appropriate allocation of assets in your portfolio. This involves determining how much of your investment should be in stocks, bonds, real estate, and other asset classes. Each class carries different risks and potential returns, influencing how your portfolio behaves under various market conditions.

Selection

With your asset allocation in place, the selection process involves choosing specific investments within each asset class. This might include selecting individual stocks, bond issues, real estate investment trusts (REITs), or commodities. The aim here is to build a collection of investments that, together, align with your investment strategy and objectives.

Execution

Execution is where plans turn into action. This step involves purchasing the chosen investments according to your asset allocation. Whether through a broker, advisor, or online platform, the key here is to follow through with your strategy, remembering that discipline is crucial for long-term success.

Monitoring and Rebalancing

The final step is ongoing monitoring and rebalancing. Keeping an eye on your investments and the broader market allows you to make informed decisions about adjustments to your portfolio. As markets move, your initial asset allocation might shift, necessitating rebalancing to stay aligned with your goals and risk tolerance. This step ensures your portfolio remains robust over time, adapting to changes in market conditions and your personal financial situation.

The PRF emphasizes a disciplined, structured approach to

building a diversified investment portfolio. Through careful planning, execution, and monitoring, investors can enhance their portfolio's ability to weather market volatility, supporting their long-term financial objectives.

These steps form the foundation of a diversified investment approach, offering a roadmap to navigating market uncertainties while aiming for sustained wealth growth.

Embracing the strategy of diversification is much like building a resilient and robust safety net. It's not merely an option for the cautious investor but a fundamental cornerstone for anyone looking to thrive in the unpredictable world of investing. As we've journeyed through the intricacies of spreading investments across various asset classes, the clear takeaway is that this approach isn't just about preserving capital—it's about positioning oneself for holistic growth.

The Foundation of Risk Mitigation

At the heart of a savvy investor's playbook is the understanding that **diversification mitigates risk**. This isn't just a safety measure; it's a strategic maneuver that sets the stage for sustainable wealth accumulation. Think of it as spreading seeds in different conditions—while not all will flourish, the diversification ensures that you're not reliant on a single crop to sustain your fields.

Crafting a Robust Investment Portfolio

Implementing effective diversification strategies goes beyond mere allocation. It's about crafting a synergy among assets, where their collective strength is greater than any individual part. This is not a one-size-fits-all template but a tailored suit that fits the unique contours of each investor's financial goals, risk tolerance, and market outlook.

Navigating Market Volatility with Confidence

Market volatility is an inherent part of investing, yet it need not be a source of sleepless nights. A well-diversified portfolio acts as a buffer, smoothing out the rough edges of market swings and providing a steadier path towards your financial goals. *It's akin to having multiple sails on your vessel, ensuring that if one catches a turbulent wind, the others will keep you on course.*

A culmination of these elements underscores the profound power of diversification. It's not merely about protection; it's about smartly positioning yourself to capture opportunities across the spectrum of asset classes. By mastering the fundamentals of investment diversification, implementing strategic portfolio decisions, and confidently navigating through market volatilities, you are laying down the tracks towards a future of financial freedom and security.

It's crucial, however, to remember that diversification is not a set-it-and-forget-it strategy. The financial markets are dynamic, and so should be your approach to diversification. Regular reviews and adjustments in response to changing market conditions, personal circumstances, and financial goals are imperative to maintaining an effective diversified portfolio.

So, as we move forward, let this chapter serve as both a guide and a reminder of the power inherent in diversification. Embrace it not just as a strategy but as a philosophy—a fundamental building block towards unlocking the doors to sustained wealth and financial independence. It's a journey well worth embarking on, with each step forward marking progress towards the ultimate destination of financial freedom.

Chapter 8: Investing for Tomorrow: The Long-Term Wealth Mindset

Ellen drew a long breath that carried the scent of a freshly mowed lawn through the open window. She stood in the quiet of her modest kitchen, fingers tracing the edge of an envelope that held within it the remnants of her late husband's retirement fund. The morning light danced across the table, casting long stripes that seemed to confine the thoughts she dared not let run wild.

From behind the gentle frame of her glasses, her eyes clouded with a vision of the years unfurling ahead, a future she must shoulder without the man who had promised to be at her side. She had been thrust into a role she had not rehearsed – that of a navigator through the choppy waters of financial stability and the guardian of a legacy meant to last a lifetime.

Her neighbor Jack, gruff but kind, hailed her from across the fence, snapping her back to reality. "Are you going to the community center later? They're talking about investment for folks our age." Ellen managed a smile that didn't quite reach her eyes, nodding in response. Jack, she thought, always had his mind wrapped tight around tomorrow's promise, while she found herself tethered to the yesterdays slipping through her fingers.

Steeling herself, Ellen sat at the worn kitchen table, documents laid bare like blueprints of a future she found herself constructing alone. Her husband's laughter used to fill the room during these mundane activities, making the dreary task of budgeting feel like an adventure for two. Now each figure on the spreadsheet felt like a stone in her pocket, pulling her deeper into waters she wasn't sure she could navigate.

She thought of the time they had scrimped and saved, focusing not on fleeting whims, but on the steadfast dream of a golden age together. They had clung to the ideology of incremental progress – slow and steady wins, they had said in unison. Now, she was left to fan the dying embers of a joint dream, igniting her own path to security amidst a fog of uncertainty.

With each tick of the clock, a wave of resolve began to build within her. The laughter of the children riding bikes outside weaved through her contemplation, a reminder that life surged forward with relentless optimism. Could she, like those young souls, cast aside the weight of doubt and pedal forward with confidence and a roadmap drawn by lessons learned and a well of inner strength she was only just beginning to understand?

Might the seeds of future stability be nestled within the careful cultivation of her long-term plans and the deliberate tending to the dreams she harbored in her heart?

The Secret to Sustainable Wealth Lies Beyond the Horizon

Let's dive straight into the heart of it: a long-term wealth accumulation mindset isn't just a preference—it's essential. In the financial realm, where the only constant is change, having a vision that stretches far into the future can be your North Star. It guides you, keeps you focused, and, most importantly, ensures that you're not just surviving but thriving amid the fluctuations. This isn't about quick wins; it's about building a foundation so solid that neither market volatility nor economic downturns can shake it. It's about **investing for tomorrow**.

The journey towards sustainable wealth is akin to planting a tree. You nurture it, protect it, and though it might not bear fruit immediately, its growth is inevitable. Cultivating a mindset focused on long-term financial stability and wealth accumulation isn't just a strategy; it's a **philosophy** of patience, consistency, and foresight. Such a mindset distinguishes between fleeting gains and lasting wealth, between the impulsive reactions of the crowd and the calculated decisions of the sage.

Now, let's get practical. Implementing strategies aimed at steady growth requires more than just a hopeful outlook; it demands action. Whether it's diversifying your investment portfolio, embracing compounding's power, or staying informed about market trends, the goal remains the same: to navigate and withstand financial uncertainties. Yes, the markets will ebb and flow, but your approach, grounded in a commitment to consistent, incremental growth, positions you to weather any storm.

Of course, setting actionable long-term financial goals is where the rubber meets the road. These aren't mere wishful thoughts but are detailed, thoughtful, and realistic objectives that prioritize sustainable wealth over fleeting gains. They're your roadmap, your guiding light, leading the way through the often murky waters of financial planning. They remind you that every step taken today is a step toward your future financial freedom.

What does this all mean in the context of amplifying your assets, as outlined in *Wealth Unlocked*? Simply put, the long-term wealth mindset is the bedrock upon which successful investing and tactical tax planning are built. It's the difference between being at the mercy of the market's whims and proactively shaping your financial destiny. By focusing on longevity over immediacy, you're not merely playing the game; you're changing it, setting the rules, and walking the path less traveled, but infinitely more rewarding.

Consider the analogy of a seasoned navigator charting a course through open seas. You wouldn't aim for the nearest landmark; you'd set your sights on distant shores, understanding that the journey there would be fraught with challenges yet also ripe with opportunity. Similarly, in investing, the allure of quick returns can often distract from the ultimate prize: enduring wealth. It's about seeing beyond the horizon, recognizing the vast potential that lies ahead, and steadfastly moving toward it.

Embrace this approach with both hands, and watch as the doors to financial security and success swing wide open. The path won't always be smooth, but the destination—lasting wealth and the freedom it brings—is worth the journey. Remember, it's not just about having enough for today but ensuring abundance for tomorrow. And that, in essence, is the key to unlocking a future replete with financial possibilities.

Cultivate a Mindset Focused on Long-Term Financial Stability and Wealth Accumulation

In the realm of financial planning, the sprinters often grab the headlines with their rapid gains, but it's the marathon runners who truly capture the essence of wealth accumulation. True financial stability doesn't come from the fleeting triumphs of short-term speculation but from the steady, disciplined approach of long-term investment. Just like building a house, a solid foundation must first be laid before the structure can rise. In investing, this foundation is built on the understanding that wealth grows over time through compounded returns, not overnight through luck or speculation.

Consider the analogy of planting a tree. When the seed is first sown, growth is imperceptible. Day by day, with proper nourishment, it sprouts and eventually grows into a sturdy tree. This process mirrors long-term investing quite closely. At first, the increments in portfolio value might seem minimal, almost frustratingly so. Yet, with patience and the right strategy, these small gains compound, leading to substantial wealth growth over time.

To shift towards a long-term wealth accumulation mindset, individuals must recognize the importance of patience and discipline. Immediate gratification is tempting; the allure of quick gains can sway even the most rational investor. However, understanding that true financial growth requires time is paramount. It's about making investments with a vision for the future, not just the immediate horizon. This involves choosing investment vehicles that align with long-term financial goals and accepting that market fluctuations are part of the journey towards achieving these goals.

Embracing a long-term perspective also means being prepared to hold investments through periods of volatility without panic-selling at a loss. Educating oneself about historical market trends and the cyclic nature of economies can bolster one's resolve during downturns. Remember, the greatest oak was once a little nut that held its ground.

Cultivating a mindset focused on long-term wealth accumulation is the bedrock of sustainable financial

success.

Implement Strategies Aimed at Steady Growth to Navigate and Withstand Financial Uncertainties

In the constantly fluctuating world of finance, steadiness often takes precedence over speed. Strategies aimed at steady growth are akin to constructing a dam designed to withstand the ebbing and flowing tides of a river. These strategies, grounded in diversification and risk management, aim to protect and gradually grow one's wealth despite the unpredictable nature of financial markets.

Diversification is not just a buzzword but a shield against the volatility of markets. By spreading investments across various asset classes, geographical locations, and industries, one can reduce the risk of catastrophic losses. It's a way to ensure that when one part of the portfolio underperforms, another might thrive, maintaining overall balance and mitigating sudden financial downturns.

Risk management, on the other hand, involves setting clear boundaries to protect against potential losses. This might include setting stop-loss orders, allocating assets based on one's risk tolerance, and regularly reviewing and adjusting one's investment portfolio to align with changing financial goals and market conditions.

Utilizing dollar-cost averaging is another strategy focused on steady growth. By investing a fixed amount regularly, regardless of the market's condition, one buys more shares when prices are low and fewer when they are high. Over time, this can potentially lower the average cost per share, a method that champions consistency over timing the market.

Imagine navigating a sailboat in the open sea. The goal is not to outpace the wind but to harness its power to steadily move towards your destination. This approach of steady, deliberate action not only builds resilience against unexpected financial storms but also encourages growth through all market conditions.

But what if this steady growth mindset was the key to unlocking not just financial security, but financial freedom as well?

Set Actionable Long-Term Financial Goals That Prioritize Sustainable Wealth Over Fleeting Gains

The journey to financial prosperity begins with setting clear, actionable long-term goals. Without a destination in mind, it's easy to drift aimlessly or chase after the mirage of quick riches. Long-term goals act as the North Star, guiding financial decisions and strategies towards sustainable wealth.

These goals should be specific, measurable, achievable,

relevant, and time-bound (SMART). Whether it's retiring by a certain age, funding a child's education, or buying a dream home, these goals provide the motivation and framework necessary for disciplined investing.

The process of setting these goals also involves a deep understanding of one's financial situation and aspirations. It requires an honest assessment of income, expenses, debts, and savings. From this foundation, achievable milestones can be set, serving as checkpoints along the path to the ultimate financial objectives.

Consider the analogy of a mountain climber. The peak represents the long-term financial goal, while the base camps are the short-term milestones. Just as climbers adjust their routes based on weather conditions and their physical state, investors must be flexible, willing to adjust their strategies in response to financial climates and personal circumstances.

By setting and working towards articulated long-term financial goals, individuals prioritize sustainable wealth that can support their lifestyle and aspirations, marking the convergence of the three key learning objectives: cultivating a long-term mindset, implementing strategies for steady growth, and setting actionable, sustainable financial goals.

Cultivating a long-term wealth mindset isn't just about setting goals; it's about transforming the way you view your financial future. It's about seeing beyond the horizon of immediate gratification and navigating towards a future brimming with financial stability and success. Remember, the journey towards long-term wealth isn't a sprint; it's a marathon. It requires patience, resilience, and a strategic approach to overcome any financial uncertainties that may come your way.

Cultivate a Long-Term Mindset

Building a foundation for long-term financial stability starts in the mind. Like planting a seed that grows into a towering tree, your mindset shapes your financial destiny. This is not just about hoping for the best; it's about making a steadfast commitment to your future self. It's about embracing the reality that *small, consistent actions taken today can lead to substantial growth over time.* Think of it like tending to a garden. Just as you wouldn't plant seeds and expect them to grow overnight, you shouldn't expect your investments to flourish without time, care, and strategic planning.

Steady Growth in Uncertain Times

Financial markets are inherently unpredictable. They ebb and flow, sometimes violently, but it's your reaction to these movements that defines your financial journey. Implementing **strategies aimed at steady growth** is akin to building a lighthouse that stands firm, guiding you through the stormy seas of market volatility. Remember, it's not about avoiding the storm but learning how to sail in it. By focusing on sustainable growth and not being swayed by the siren calls of short-term gains, you're setting a course towards true financial freedom.

Sustainable Wealth Over Fleeting Gains

Setting actionable long-term financial goals is critical. But let's be clear, this isn't about vague aspirations or wishful thinking. It's about defining what sustainable wealth means to you and crafting a clear, achievable path to get there. Imagine you're on a road trip. Without a map or a destination in mind, you're simply driving aimlessly. But with a clear destination and a roadmap, you navigate with purpose, making adjustments as needed, but always moving forward. That's the essence of setting long-term financial goals. It's about having a vision that guides your decisions and keeps you on track, even when the unexpected happens.

The Path Ahead

As we've explored, adopting a long-term wealth mindset is the cornerstone of financial success. It's not always easy, and there will be times when your resolve is tested. However, by staying committed to your goals, employing strategies for steady growth, and focusing on sustainable wealth, you'll navigate the complexities of the financial landscape with greater ease and confidence. Remember, the choices you make today shape your financial future. By keeping your eyes on the horizon and your hands steady at the helm, you're not just investing in your future—you're securing it. Let's embrace this journey with both the seriousness it demands and the optimism it deserves.

Chapter 9: Decoding the Market: Research Driven Investing

In the dim light of a modest study, a gentle clock ticked the late afternoon into early evening. Samuel leaned back in his chair, rubbing his eyes, the glow of his computer screen washing over countless charts and graphs. Two decades had sculpted him into a shape that fit comfortably in the world of finance, his intuition sharpened by the countless ebbs and flows of market tides.

This evening, though, a restlessness stirred in his chest, a nagging whisper of opportunity he couldn't quite silence. He thought of the container ships he'd seen while walking along the quay that morning, emblematic of the global trade that fueled his every decision. The scent of salt and diesel had underlined the bustle of commerce, and whispers from the market spoke of shifting patterns, of economies awakening from slumber.

Samuel sifted through the data, the numbers a tapestry woven from the threads of human endeavor. He knew that somewhere within—hidden between the unemployment rates inching downward and the consumer confidence creeping up—lay the secrets that would herald the next boon. He recalled the excitement, the adrenaline rush of grasping the tail of a fleeting trend, leveraging it into prosperity.

A soft sound drew his gaze to the window, where evening light fought a losing battle against the advancing night. He paused, considering the fragility of their gains, of his gains. They were alike, the day and his fortunes, both subject to the inexorable passage of time. A laugh shook loose from deep within him—the markets, after all, were not governed by the turning of the earth but by the hearts and minds of people, capricious and unpredictable.

Outside, city lights flickered on, mirroring the stars above, a reminder of the constancy amidst change. With each light, a family, an individual, decisions and worries, futures hinging on the whims of an unpredictable market. There was solace in the research, in the numbers and charts that seemed to whisper secrets of a future not yet written. They were Samuel's steady companions in a world where chance played a hand in every human affair.

Silence enveloped the room as the screen blinked off, and Samuel stood, stretching. For a moment, he remained still, contemplating the days ahead. He understood that the choices he'd make would be less about divining the future and more about navigating the shifting sands of the present. But, could he, a solitary man in his quiet study, tease out the market's whispers and turn them into a symphony of success?

Unlock the Power of Market Analysis

The world of investing might seem like uncharted waters to the uninitiated, but to those who master the art of market analysis, it's a sea rich with opportunity. This insight isn't just for seasoned investors; it's a golden key for anyone looking to amplify their assets. The journey toward financial freedom isn't a game of chance; it's a strategic path paved with informed decisions, comprehensive research, and an understanding of market dynamics.

Imagine navigating the financial markets with a map and compass—this is what effective market research offers. It's not about making predictions; it's about making informed choices. **Conducting thorough market analysis** isn't just a good practice; it's the backbone of successful investing. It's how you uncover hidden gems, those investment opportunities that others might overlook because they're not digging deep enough.

But where do you start? It begins with **utilizing economic indicators and market trends**. These are not just numbers and graphs; they're the story of what's happening on a global scale, told in a language that, once understood, offers invaluable insights. These indicators can guide you, showing when to hold back and when to dive in. They are the weather vane of the financial world, and by learning to read them, you're setting yourself up not just to succeed, but to excel.

You might wonder how all this minimizes risk. It's simple, yet profoundly effective: **Informed decision-making based on comprehensive research** drastically reduces the chances of making misguided investment choices. It's the difference between gambling and investing. The former is hoping luck is on your side, while the latter is ensuring you've stacked the odds in your favor as much as possible. Minimizing risks doesn't mean avoiding them altogether; it means understanding them so well that you can navigate through or around them.

This journey of market analysis is not a solitary one. It's a dialogue between you and the world's economic movements. It requires curiosity, dedication, and a willingness to learn. Each piece of data, each trend analysis, brings you closer to making investment choices that are not just good, but exceptional. It's about honing your ability to see potential where others see complexity.

The landscape of investing is ever-changing, and so must our strategies be. **Economic indicators and market trends** are not static; they are as dynamic as the markets themselves. Staying attuned to these changes is what separates successful investors from the rest. This doesn't mean being swayed by every wind of change but understanding which trends have the potential to impact your investment decisions meaningfully.

The path to financial freedom is not a straight line; it's a series of informed decisions, each building on the last. By embracing market research, analysis, and strategic planning, you're not just investing in the market; you're investing in yourself. This chapter is designed to guide you through that process, offering the tools, insights, and strategies necessary to navigate the complexities of the financial world with confidence.

Remember, the goal isn't just to survive the unpredictable nature of the markets; it's to thrive within them. With thorough research, a deep understanding of economic indicators, and strategic decision-making, you're not just unlocking wealth; you're unlocking potential—yours and the market's. Let this journey of discovery begin, leading you not just to financial success but to a deeper understanding of the intricate world of investing.

Navigating the Ocean of Opportunity: Market Analysis Unveiled

Conducting a thorough market analysis is akin to preparing for a sea voyage in search of undiscovered lands rich with treasures. Just as a seasoned captain wouldn't set sail without a detailed map, an investor must not dive into the vast ocean of financial markets without a comprehensive understanding of the current tides and winds. This understanding begins with recognizing the importance of delving deep into market data to uncover hidden investment opportunities that promise substantial rewards.

The foundation of successful investment strategies lies in gathering and analyzing a wide range of market data. This includes historical price movements, volume trends, and financial statements of potential investment targets. By scrutinizing this data, investors can identify patterns that guide them towards making informed decisions. It's not merely about crunching numbers; it's about interpreting what those numbers tell us about the future health and prospects of businesses and the broader market.

Imagine a miner panning for gold in a river. Not every rock in the pan will be gold; similarly, not every investment opportunity uncovered during market analysis will be worth pursuing. But just as the miner uses his pan and sieve to separate gold from mere stones, this meticulous process of analysis helps investors differentiate between a potentially lucrative investment and a financial mirage.

An integral part of market analysis is understanding the context in which companies operate. This involves keeping an eye on industry trends, regulatory changes, and macroeconomic factors that could affect market dynamics. By considering these external factors, investors can develop a more nuanced view of potential investments, enabling them to make decisions not just based on financial data but also on the broader picture of how different forces interact in the market.

In summary, thorough market analysis is the compass by which savvy investors navigate the complex seas of

investment opportunities.

Deciphering Economic Signals: The Art of Making Informed Choices

The role of economic indicators and market trends in guiding investment decisions cannot be overstated. These indicators, much like the weather forecasts for a sailor, provide essential insights into the future economic climate. Understanding these signals allows investors to adjust their sails accordingly, ensuring their investment portfolio is not caught in a storm but is instead riding the favorable winds of growth.

Interest rates, inflation, unemployment figures, and GDP growth are a few of the many economic indicators that paint a picture of the market's overall health. These indicators help investors decipher the economic story unfolding before them, revealing chapters of expansion or cautionary tales of impending downturns. By integrating this economic narrative with market trends, investors can forecast potential shifts in market sentiment and position their investments to capitalize on these movements.

Consider how a gardener must understand the seasons to plant and harvest effectively. In the same vein, investors use economic indicators and market trends to determine the right time to 'plant' new investments or 'harvest' returns. It's a dynamic process, requiring constant vigilance and adaptability as economic conditions change.

Economic indicators and market trends do not operate in isolation; they are interconnected in a complex web of cause and effect. For instance, rising interest rates often lead to higher borrowing costs, affecting consumer spending and business investments. Recognizing these interdependencies is crucial for developing a comprehensive investment strategy that anticipates rather than reacts to market shifts.

Incorporating economic indicators and market trends into investment decisions allows investors to adopt a proactive approach. Rather than being swept away by market volatility, informed investors can navigate through turbulence with confidence, making strategic choices that align with their financial goals and risk tolerance.

Could understanding these economic signals be the key to unlocking your path to financial success?

Mastering the Balancing Act: Risk Management Through Research

Minimizing risks and enhancing portfolio returns in the complex world of investing is akin to a tightrope walker maintaining their balance. Just as the performer uses a balancing pole to navigate the precarious line, investors leverage comprehensive research to find equilibrium between potential risks and rewards. Armed with in-depth market insights, they can make informed decisions that carefully weigh the upside potential against potential pitfalls.

The cornerstone of risk management is diversification. By spreading investments across various asset classes, industries, and geographical regions, investors can mitigate the impact of a downturn in any single area on their overall portfolio. However, effective diversification demands more than just random selection; it requires a strategic approach informed by thorough research and analysis. Understanding the nuances and correlations between different investments enables investors to construct a well-balanced portfolio that is resilient in the face of market volatility.

Imagine crafting a mosaic where each piece represents a different investment. Just as the beauty and integrity of the mosaic depend on how well the pieces fit together, the strength and potential of an investment portfolio rely on the synergistic relationship between its diverse components. Through diligent research, investors identify which pieces complement each other, creating a harmonious and robust financial picture.

At the heart of informed decision-making is the continuous monitoring and analysis of existing investments and market conditions. This proactive approach ensures that investors can respond swiftly to changes, seizing opportunities for growth while minimizing exposure to undue risk. Whether it's recognizing the signs of an emerging market trend or identifying the early indicators of a potential downturn, comprehensive research provides the insights needed for timely and effective action.

Harnessing the power of comprehensive market analysis, economic indicators, and insightful research forms the triad for informed investment decisions, enabling investors to minimize risks while maximizing portfolio returns.

Navigating the complex terrain of the investment world requires more than just a passive approach. **Conducting thorough market analysis and research** is akin to preparing for a voyage across uncharted waters. As an investor, your map and compass are the valuable insights gleaned from economic indicators, market trends, and rigorous analysis. These tools empower you to chart a course through the volatile seas of the market, steering toward opportunities that others might miss and away from unseen risks.

Understanding the Current to Navigate the Future

Imagine for a moment that the financial market is a vast ocean. In this ocean, currents represent the economic indicators and market trends that guide the movements of investment opportunities—much like fish in the sea. An adept fisherman knows where to cast his nets by reading these currents; similarly, **a savvy investor uses these indicators to inform strategic investment choices**. This doesn't necessarily mean predicting the future with certainty but rather understanding the present with clarity.

What's crucial is the ability to distill complex information into actionable insights. This could mean spotting a trend in consumer behavior that points to a burgeoning market or identifying indicators that suggest a potential downturn. Through informed decision-making, you're not just reacting to the market's fluctuations; you're anticipating them, minimizing risks, and enhancing your portfolio's returns.

Minimizing Risks Through Informed Decision-Making

Risks are an inherent part of investing, but they can be intelligently managed. Think of it as preparing for a storm; you don't wait until it hits to seek shelter. By *thoroughly researching and understanding the market*, you're building your investment portfolio's resilience against the unpredictable elements of the market. This doesn't mean avoiding all risks but rather assessing them with a judicious eye, balancing potential rewards against potential losses.

Strategic diversification is one aspect of this risk management. It's the idea of not putting all your eggs in one basket but spreading them out. This way, if one investment encounters a challenge, the stability of your entire portfolio isn't compromised. By weaving together a tapestry of investments based on comprehensive market analysis, you create a buffer against the volatility of individual assets.

Harnessing the Power of Research for Future Success

Your journey in the investment landscape is ongoing, and the terrain is ever-changing. As such, *the cultivation of a research-driven investment strategy is not a one-time effort but a continuous process.* It demands curiosity, diligence, and a commitment to lifelong learning. The world of investments doesn't stand still, and neither should you. By staying informed and agile, adjusting your strategies in response to new information and market dynamics, you're not just surviving in the market; you're thriving.

Embracing a research-driven approach is empowering. It enables you to navigate the complexities of the financial world with confidence and savvy. Remember, the most successful investors are not those who rely on luck but those who are prepared. By **making informed investment decisions based on comprehensive research**, you're ensuring that your investment portfolio doesn't just weather the storms but sails forward toward your financial goals.

Let's embark on this journey with the rigor and passion it deserves. Your path to unlocking wealth and achieving financial freedom is paved with the stones of knowledge, research, and strategic action. Together, let's chart a course toward a prosperous future.

Chapter 10: Empowerment Through Expertise: Navigating Financial Complexities with Confidence

The sun beat down unforgivingly onto the cracked pavement of Vine Street, where Jonathan found himself walking, a slight furrow to his brow that mirrored the scores upon the ground. He carried himself with the weight of decisions, vast and unseen, tucked like so many notes into the briefcase swung in his hand. It wasn't just investments he mused over, but life choices, branching like the great oaks in Hyde Park, each limb a future he could climb.

He paused before the diner, its windows steamed from the heat of the grill and the breath of regulars leaning into their morning routines. Jonathan peered inside, absent-mindedly fixing his windswept tie, his reflection tangled with the images of waitresses gliding from table to table, the clatter of dishes an erratic symphony to those who hunger they rushed to sate. The clinks were coins in a jar, each a reminder of the fiscal prudence he sought to instill in his own life, the very advice he now needed distilled from the cacophony of economic debate.

Beneath the hum of the city, his mind grappled with the higher echelons of monetary strategy. This was not about scrimping on lattes or stowing away loose change, but about a surgical strike into the heart of his financial landscape. A fusion of expert insight and his own intimate knowledge would be crucial. And amid the chimes of the city, Jonathan felt the pulse of an opportunity, the beating heart of the stock market whispering through the fiber of his being.

He stepped into the shadow of a building, its façade a chessboard of windows and stonework, where men and women pondered moves and countermoves behind reflective glass. A cool draft swirled around him, carrying the musk of city life. Like the shifting breeze, Jonathan knew he needed to navigate the complexities with agility and precision. Overhead, a mechanical bird soared, a silver streak against the blue—an airplane charting its course just as he plotted his.

It was at moments like this, when the city fell into a lull just before the lunchtime crescendo, that Jonathan could almost touch the tendrils of the future. He envisioned his goals, seemingly so distant yet maddeningly close—a life unmarred by financial uncertainty, where each decision bore the ripe fruit of his labor and strategy. He held onto this vision, as tangible as the leather of his briefcase, and as delicate as the dreams it represented.

Does the quiet confidence in his step reveal a man well on his way to triumph, or do the ghosts of doubt still linger beneath the sheen of a practiced smile?

Unlocking Financial Expertise: Your Key to a Wealthier Tomorrow

In the labyrinth of financial decision-making, navigating with precision and confidence is not just optional—it's essential. As you stand on the brink of making choices that will shape your financial future, the importance of expert guidance tailored to your unique journey cannot be overstressed. The reality is, the landscape of wealth-building is as intricate as it is volatile. Without a map drawn by those who have traversed its peaks and valleys, it's easy to lose your way. **Empowerment through expertise** is not merely a choice; it's the cornerstone of achieving advanced financial goals.

This chapter is dedicated to guiding you through the complexities of the financial landscape with a sure-footed approach. We've reached a pivot in our wealth-building saga, where the theoretical meets the practical. Here, you'll learn to **leverage expert insights and tailored advice** to make decisions that align with your sophisticated objectives. It's about moving beyond a foundational understanding of asset amplification, stepping into the arena of advanced decision-making with the confidence of a seasoned strategist.

The pivot around which this discussion turns is not just about acquiring knowledge; it's about applying it. With actionable strategies designed to meet your fiscal goals, you will be equipped to **overcome challenges** that once seemed insurmountable. Whether it's mastering savvy investing or tactical tax planning, the insights from seasoned experts serve as invaluable tools in your arsenal. These strategies are more than just tips; they are a framework for action—a pathway carved in the bedrock of professional experience and success.

Taking control of your financial future is an empowering step, one that involves a deepened understanding and command of the financial landscape. It's akin to learning a new language, where fluency comes from both study and practice. By delving into the nuances of mutual funds, option securities, convertible debentures, and real estate investments, not to mention advanced tax strategies, you're doing more than just preparing for the future. **You're shaping it.**

As we tie together the threads of our earlier discussions, we elevate the conversation to focus on long-term success. This journey through the intricacies of financial growth shines a light on the core problem many face: navigating a complex financial landscape to build substantial wealth. But with the right tools and understanding, the path becomes clear. The strategies detailed in earlier chapters, from developing a robust real estate portfolio to leveraging advanced tax solutions and investing in a variety of vehicles, are your stepping stones.

Remember, **mastering innovative wealth-building**

strategies is not an insurmountable task reserved for the few. It's achievable within 1 to 2 years, given the right guidance and determination. As we culminate our discussion, keep in mind that the journey to financial freedom doesn't end here. It evolves with every decision, every risk taken, and every goal achieved.

The keys to unlocking your financial potential lie within these pages. They serve not just as a guide but as a dialogue—one that invites you to question, to explore, and ultimately, to succeed. As you turn these insights into action, remember that empowerment through expertise is your foundation. With it, you can navigate the complexities of the financial landscape and embrace your financial future with a sense of purpose and confidence. *This is not the end, but a new beginning.*

Navigating the world of finance, especially at an advanced stage, requires more than just basic knowledge; it necessitates a deep dive into expert insights and bespoke advice. Imagine setting sail in the vast ocean with just a rudimentary map. Without a seasoned navigator or a finely-tuned compass, the journey becomes fraught with uncertainty. This metaphor mirrors the need for expert-backed guidance in financial decision-making - the compass being the tailored insights from those who've traversed these waters before.

Every investment opportunity or tax-saving strategy comes with its unique set of challenges and benefits. To understand these nuances, one must look beyond generic advice.

Financial experts, with their years of experience and keen insight, offer advice that's not just valuable but tailored to individual financial situations. Like a tailor who measures twice but cuts once, experts measure multiple variables before suggesting a plan of action. This precision ensures that decisions made are not just good but *ideal* for the individual.

In an ever-evolving financial landscape, staying updated with the latest trends and regulations is not just beneficial; it's essential. However, the sheer volume of information available can be overwhelming. Expert insights serve as a filter, distilling complex information into digestible, actionable advice. Much like a chef skillfully combines ingredients to create a dish that's more than the sum of its parts, financial experts combine their knowledge of market trends, regulatory changes, and economic indicators to offer advice that's robust, relevant, and timely.

The beauty of tailored advice lies in its specificity and applicability. It moves beyond the one-size-fits-all approach, recognizing that each individual's financial goals, risk tolerance, and life circumstances are unique. Tailored advice considers these factors to offer strategies that are not only effective but also achievable. This level of personalization empowers individuals, giving them the clarity and confidence needed to make decisions that align with their long-term financial ambitions.

The key takeaway: Leveraging expert insights and tailored

advice is not just advantageous; it's fundamental for advanced financial decision-making.

Overcome Challenges with Sophisticated Strategies

In the realm of personal finance, encountering challenges is a given. Resolving these challenges, however, is not about brute force but employing sophisticated strategies designed for complex fiscal goals. It's akin to navigating a dense forest; the path isn't always clear, but with the right tools and guidance, one can find a way through. This is where sophisticated strategies come into play, acting as the compass guiding you through the financial wilderness.

The beauty of actionable strategies is their capacity to transform challenges into stepping stones. Whether it's market volatility, tax implications, or investment risks, each challenge presents an opportunity to refine goals, reassess strategies, and advance toward financial objectives. It's the strategic application of knowledge, combined with timely action, that turns financial obstacles into milestones of achievement.

Consider for a moment the intricacies of tax planning. Without a nuanced strategy, one might see taxation as a mere hindrance to wealth accumulation. However, sophisticated tax planning strategies can turn this around, leveraging tax laws to not only minimize liability but also to enhance financial growth. It's about seeing beyond the immediate challenge to the potential benefits that savvy planning can unlock.

Empowering oneself with sophisticated strategies goes beyond mere knowledge acquisition; it's about application. It's one thing to know about diverse investment vehicles or tax-saving mechanisms, but it's another to apply these strategies effectively. This is where the true challenge lies. However, with persistence, a willingness to learn, and adapt, overcoming these challenges becomes not just possible but probable.

Imagine seeing your financial goals materialize not despite the challenges but because of them. This transformation occurs when sophisticated strategies are employed with precision and foresight. It's not simply a matter of choosing the right investments or saving enough; it's about aligning those choices with long-term objectives and current fiscal realities.

Could the key to unlocking your financial potential lie in viewing challenges not as barriers, but as beacons guiding you toward sophisticated strategies?

Commanding the Financial Landscape

Taking control of one's financial future isn't merely about making informed decisions today; it's about continuously evolving one's understanding and command of the complex financial landscape. Imagine each financial decision as a brushstroke on the canvas of your financial future. Individually, these strokes might seem insignificant, but together, they create a masterpiece that's both beautiful and uniquely yours.

This deepened understanding isn't acquired overnight; it's cultivated through persistent learning, deliberate action, and strategic patience. The financial landscape, with its constant fluctuations and shifts, demands not just attentiveness but a willingness to adapt and learn. Just as a sailor must understand the sea's moods and maneuver accordingly, an individual must grasp the nuances of the financial market to navigate it successfully.

A commanding knowledge of the financial landscape enables individuals to anticipate changes, act proactively, and mitigate risks efficiently. It's about having a bird's eye view of the terrain while also being adept at navigating the minutiae. This dual perspective ensures that decisions are made not just based on current trends but with an understanding of their long-term impact.

Empowering oneself with this level of understanding brings not only financial gains but also peace of mind. Knowing that each decision is made with a deep comprehension of the financial ecosystem instills a sense of confidence that is immeasurable. It transforms financial planning from a task to a journey—one that's navigated with wisdom and foresight.

Empowering readers with tailored expert advice, actionable strategies, and a commanding understanding of the financial landscape enables them to navigate

financial complexities with confidence, ensuring long-term success.

Empowering yourself through the mastery of financial complexities is not just about accumulating wealth; it's about fostering a profound sense of confidence and control over your financial destiny. By leveraging expert insights and tailored advice, you step into a realm of advanced decision-making, setting the stage for achieving ambitious fiscal objectives. This journey is both enlightening and empowering, revealing the full spectrum of opportunities that sophisticated financial strategies offer.

Leverage Expert Insights

The dynamism of today's financial landscape necessitates a partnership with those who navigate its intricacies daily. **Specialized guidance** is more than a luxury; it's a fundamental resource that illuminates the path toward your financial goals. Imagine standing at the helm of a ship, with seasoned navigators charting the course. Their insights aren't merely suggestions; they're the compass by which you steer, ensuring you're not only avoiding the common pitfalls but are on the fastest route to your desired destination. Tailoring this advice to your unique situation transforms complexity into clarity, enabling informed, confident decision-making.

Overcome Challenges with Actionable

Strategies

Every investor's journey is interspersed with challenges. But with the right strategies, these challenges become mere stepping stones rather than insurmountable barriers. **Actionable strategies** designed for sophisticated goals equip you to face financial hurdles with assurance. It's like navigating a complex maze with a map that highlights the quickest exits. This proactive approach turns potential setbacks into valuable learning experiences, ensuring continuous progress toward your financial objectives.

Take Control with Deepened Understanding

At the heart of financial empowerment is a **deep understanding** of the economic landscape. This isn't about superficial familiarity with investment vehicles or tax strategies. It's about acquiring a profound command of the financial world's nuances, enabling a proactive and informed stance on wealth building. Consider it akin to becoming fluent in a new language; suddenly, you're not just following along—you're engaging, interpreting, and influencing with confidence. This level of understanding puts you in the driver's seat of your financial journey, ensuring that every decision propels you closer to your goals.

In weaving through the chapters of this guide, you've embarked on a transformative journey, culminating in the realization that the key to unlocking your financial potential lies in the sophisticated strategies and nuanced understanding put forth. From mastering diverse investment vehicles to navigating advanced tax solutions, you've unlocked the tools to not only build substantial wealth within 1 to 2 years but to do so with the confidence and clarity that comes from being deeply informed.

Remember, the journey to financial freedom is both an art and a science—requiring creativity in strategy implementation and precision in decision-making. These principles come alive when applied with a deep understanding of the financial world, ensuring that the complexity of the market becomes a playground for innovation rather than a labyrinth of confusion.

As you move forward, armed with the knowledge and strategies discussed, let your journey be guided by the confidence that comes from expertise. Let the challenges you face not deter but inspire you, as each step brings you closer to the financial freedom you seek. By embracing the actionable strategies, tailored advice, and deep understanding offered, you're not just navigating the financial landscape; you're reshaping it to fit your vision of success.

Embark with confidence, knowing that you possess the tools, insights, and strategies to transform your financial future. The mastery of your financial destiny is not just a possibility—it's within your grasp.

Epilogue

Unlocking the Final Gate to Your Financial Freedom

Imagine standing before the vast expanse of your financial future, the key to unlocking unimaginable wealth firmly in your grasp. This vision isn't just a fleeting dream but a tangible reality that's within your reach. The journey through this book has been akin to navigating a labyrinth, each chapter a turn bringing you closer to the ultimate prize: financial freedom. And here we stand, at the precipice of a new beginning, armed with knowledge, strategies, and the courage to take that final step.

The principles and strategies discussed here are designed for application in the real world, where the terrain is unpredictable yet ripe with opportunity. The keys to amplifying your assets, mastering the art of savvy investing, and the craft of tactical tax planning have been laid bare for you to seize and incorporate into the fabric of your financial plans. You've been equipped with the tools to navigate today's economic environment, adapting and thriving amidst its challenges.

Recall the cornerstone philosophies that guide this journey: Invest wisely, not only with your finances but in your continuous education and understanding of the market's ebbs and flows. Optimize your tax situation not as a mere afterthought but as a pivotal aspect of your financial strategy. Realize that real estate isn't just about location but about smart, strategic maneuvers that turn ordinary assets into extraordinary sources of income.

It's time to put this newfound knowledge into action. Start by revising your current financial plan, weaving in the advanced investment tactics and tax strategies you've learned. Experiment with diversification, not just across asset classes but within them. Play the long game in real estate, and remember the power of compounding interest in your securities investments. Consider setting up consultations with financial advisors or tax planners armed with your specific questions, ensuring that you're not just going along with generic advice but tailoring it to your unique financial landscape.

As we conclude this journey, it's critical to acknowledge that the path to financial enlightenment is ongoing. The market will evolve, laws will change, and new opportunities will emerge. Stay curious, stay vigilant, and let the principles and strategies you've learned be your compass.

Let this not be the end but a beginning to a future where you are not just a participant in your financial destiny but the master of it. Go forth with confidence, knowing that the keys to unlocking your wealth are not just in your hands but in your actions from this day forward.

Let the words of Warren Buffett inspire you as you embark on this journey: "Someone is sitting in the shade today because someone planted a tree a long time ago." Your efforts in the present are the seeds of your financial freedom tomorrow. Let them grow with wisdom, patience, and the strategic insight you now possess.

www.ingramcontent.com/pod-product-compliance
Lightning Source LLC
Chambersburg PA
CBHW050304230526
45471CB00005B/2013